DISCERNING GOD'S PURPOSE

A FATHER'S JOURNEY FROM TRAGEDY TO TRIUMPH

JIM KENNEDY

DISCERNING GOD'S PURPOSE
A FATHER'S JOURNEY FROM TRAGEDY TO TRIUMPH
Copyright © 2016 by Jim Kennedy. All rights reserved.

No part of this publication can be reproduced or transmitted in any form or by any means, electronic or mechanical, without permission in writing from the author or publisher. All Bible quotations are from the English Standard Version.

ISBN: 978-0-9984474-0-7

To My Family
Past, Present, and Future

TABLE OF CONTENTS

Introduction	1
Recognizing My Purpose	5
Chapter 1: Road Trip, 7	
Chapter 2: 911, 10	
Chapter 3: Joy to Sorrow, 12	
Chapter 4: Hope, 28	
Chapter 5: Establishing a Relationship with God, 32	
Understanding My Purpose	43
Chapter 6: Going Home, 45	
Chapter 7: Seeking Wisdom, 50	
Chapter 8: Understanding What Is Important, 58	
Chapter 9: Having Courage, 66	
Chapter 10: Don't Settle, 75	
Living In My Purpose	89
Chapter 11: The Move to Texas, 91	
Chapter 12: Restoration, 99	
Chapter 13: St. Vincent, 111	
Chapter 14: Meeting Lezroy And Neilah, 118	
Chapter 15: It's Official, 124	
Chapter 16: A New Purpose, 133	
A New Calling	153
Chapter 17: Revenge, 155	
Chapter 18: A Season of Change, 162	
Chapter 19: Having Faith, 176	
Chapter 20: A New Chapter, 181	
Conclusion: Coming Full Circle	191
Appendix	195
Acknowledgements	197

TABLE OF CONTENTS

Acknowledgements 197
Small Group Study Guide 203
    Lesson: Leaders Must Be Led, 205
    Lesson: Expect the Best, 207
    Lesson: Be Accountable for your own actions, 209
    Lesson: Don't settle for anything less than God's best, 211
    Lesson: Embrace Change, 213
    Lesson: Remember to serve others first, 215
    Lesson: Seek Wisdom, 217
    Lesson: Have Courage, 219
    Lesson: Integrity comes first, 221
    Lesson: Be Passionate about your path, 223

INTRODUCTION

I often read that experience is the best teacher. In the case of leadership development, I certainly find this to be the case. My career has spanned over twenty-eight years, with much of it being in leadership and management. At first, I will admit that I wasn't that great of a leader (OK, I sucked). There, I said it. I had training on what to do and could give orders with the best of them, but a key component was missing. I couldn't put my finger on it until I experienced adversity in a truly personal way. I often say that I've had leadership titles for most of my life but didn't truly become a leader until I became a parent. At first, I tried to manage children as if they were my employees at work. I tried to impose my will on them and promised dire consequences if things didn't go my way. Needless to say, that didn't go over so well. When things went wrong, I couldn't fire my children, nor could I fire teachers, caregivers, their friends, or others who were involved in their lives on a daily basis. Very quickly, I learned that *things* are managed, but *people* must be led. Instead of giving orders, I learned to teach and, through the art of influence, led my children down the path of life where they (and I) wanted to go.

INTRODUCTION

Another key piece of my development was learning to be led. I don't know everything. I needed a place to go where I could seek answers regarding the direction of my life. That came about when I developed my relationship with God. Like most people, I thought that I could weather the storms of life by myself until one day when I found myself in a very difficult position and needed to call on Him for help. Since that time, my development as a person and a leader has been hand in hand with that of my spiritual growth. I wouldn't be the person that I am today without God. He has given me the confidence to be able to face any situation and come out victorious on the other side.

I have read more books on leadership and management than I care to count. Walk into any bookstore and there are countless books on the shelves that discuss the latest theories on this topic. There are many people who are much more qualified than I am to do that. I wanted to write this book simply to share my story on how I came to discover my purpose in life, which in turn led to a new calling that enabled me to become the leader that I was meant to be. I can't say that I am the leader of a Fortune 500 company, but I can say that I am the leader of my family in our walk with Christ, and to me, that is worth more than silver and gold. I would love to be able to say that this book is entirely about me and my journey toward my purpose. Unfortunately, that wouldn't be true. I am blessed to go on this journey through life with an amazing wife, wonderful children, loving parents, and an extensive network of family and friends who have offered invaluable help along the way. That being said, I'm going to be honest and say that this journey is often messy and at times not a whole lot of fun; however, it was a necessary in understanding my particular assignment in life. I didn't write this book for kudos or a pat on the back but to explain how God used a very difficult situation to reveal my purpose in life that ultimately lead to a new calling. I am not unique. What He did for me is something that He can also do for you. God uses everyday situations to speak to people and to move them toward the person that they were created to be. Eventually, God is going to use something in your life to reveal your purpose to you. All you have to do is open your heart and mind—and listen.

Most parents will agree that raising children can test people in every way possible. I have three children with very different personalities who approach life in completely different ways. My oldest daughter's favorite thing is to ask the question "why" (about everything); my son likes to do things his way first and then ask questions later; and my youngest daughter is slow and methodical in her thinking because at times, she can be unsure of herself and doesn't like to make mistakes. At times I may question their approach but not their motive. One of the things that I love about them is that they always want to do their best. As a parent, that's all I can ask for. Dealing with these personalities and unique needs can at times drive us up a wall, but it is in these moments that we learned what true leadership is all about—encouraging and helping people to be their best. We learned to lead and guide through influence in order to help our children accomplish their goals. As I learned these lessons at home, I became much more tolerant and understanding toward colleagues and subordinates, which made

INTRODUCTION

me a better leader at work. All I can say is that it all started when I discovered my purpose.

It is often said that what doesn't kill you makes you stronger, and my story is a true testament to that fact. Leaders are not only responsible for developing themselves but also to help others who surround them. That is a key reason for me writing this book. I'll say that my journey doesn't start off in some nice, neat package but with the tragedy of losing two children. While watching a third fight for her life, I found the one true friend who eased my pain and was key in helping me to discover my purpose. Later, He fulfilled His promise of restoration by sending two new children into my life. He taught me the true meaning of leadership by blessing me with an opportunity to serve a cause that was greater than myself, and in doing so, gave my life a whole new meaning which in turn led me to my true calling. My prayer is that in reading about my journey, He will allow you to discover your purpose as well.

RECOGNIZING MY PURPOSE

We all have a purpose. If you didn't, you would be dead. In the Bible, the Book of Proverbs was written by King Solomon, widely credited with being one of the wisest men who walked the face of this earth. As the son of King David, God appears to Solomon in a dream after his father's death and asks what He can do for him. Without hesitation, Solomon asks for wisdom to rule over his people in a fair and just manner, and God grants his request. Solomon writes that God has a purpose for everyone; however, it is up to each of us to discover our purpose. In Proverbs 20:5, Solomon writes: "The purposes of a person's heart are deep waters, but one who has insight draws them out." When I was young, I thought that my purpose was to make money and to take care of my family. Unfortunately, it took a tragic event for God to get my attention so that He could ultimately reveal my purpose.

CHAPTER 1
ROAD TRIP

This year for our family vacation, we took a two-week trip back east to visit family. We live in Austin, Texas, and since the majority of our family lives on the East Coast, we only get to see them once or twice a year. With a family of five, road trips are an economical way of traveling so that is what we planned to do. Most of the time when we travel back home, we usually are on a tight schedule because of work or school commitments, so we don't have time to visit extended family. This year, since we were traveling in the summer and had more flexibility in our work schedules, we were not as rushed as in years past. Now that the kids are a little older, we planned this trip as a family in order to incorporate some of the places that they wanted to visit. We wanted to take the opportunity to see places that the kids may have only read about in history books as a way to expand their outlook and understanding of America. Also, since our oldest daughter will be a high school junior in the fall, it was time to start visiting colleges and universities that she wanted to consider attending after graduation.

One of the places that we were scheduled to visit is Cincinnati, Ohio. It has a special significance for us because that is where our oldest daughter was born. We left Cincinnati when she was

CHAPTER 1

three years old and hadn't been back since. For years, she has been asking to visit Cincinnati, and for years we said, "no." Part of the reason has been a busy schedule, and part of it has to do with opening up wounds from the past. Nevertheless, she asked to go, and since we had time and it wasn't too far out of the way, we added it to the list. Two days after school ended for the year, we loaded up the van, closed up the house, and hit the road.

I usually like to get an early start when driving, but with three kids and a wife who absolutely hates long drives, we didn't leave the house until two in the afternoon. As I get older, I tend to get tired if I drive late at night, but since I was trying to make it to Memphis, Tennessee before stopping to rest, I did what I had to do. We spent a short night at the Embassy Suites in Memphis, and by late morning we were back on the road and headed toward Cincinnati. Everyone was still tired from the previous day so they took the opportunity to get in some sleep time. Pretty soon, I was the only one awake in the car and was alone with my thoughts. We were passing through Nashville when I heard Dave Ramsey on the radio. He is a popular author and radio host who dispenses advice on various financial topics. This day, he was advising a caller on the wisdom of having a rainy day fund not only for emergencies but also for peace of mind. After the call ended, he told his listeners the story of how his grandmother created her own emergency fund: a jar that sat in the kitchen with the letters "GOK" or God Only Knows written on the label. Ramsey likes to say that in life, a little rain will always fall, and a rainy day fund is a good way to deal with the storms of life. He says that people often come up to him and say that he needs to be more positive in advising people how to get out of debt. He likes to joke that he is positive that it is going to rain, and people need to have a rainy day fund in order to stay out of debt. It is a joke that I had heard him say many times before, and it always brings a smile to my face. This particular day, however, the joke takes on a different meaning. I was headed to a place where I encountered one of the greatest storms of my life. I didn't have a rainy day fund when I started, but I had that and more by the time I finished, one which gave my life new meaning. It happened almost seventeen years ago, but I remember it as if it were yesterday.

Discerning God's Purpose

CHAPTER 2
911

I discovered God's purpose for my life in 1999 at Good Samaritan Hospital in Cincinnati, Ohio. My wife, Renita, was pregnant with triplets and was in her twenty-fourth week of pregnancy. This was our first pregnancy, so we were very focused on doing everything that her doctor recommended to ensure a safe pregnancy. She had her regular checkups and everything up to this point was proceeding normally (as normal as things can be for a triplet pregnancy). During the first few months, her doctor allowed her to continue to work her normal schedule but as the pregnancy progressed, she gradually had to cut back on her hours and then finally the doctor put her on bed rest as a precaution.

When she started to dilate early, her doctor performed a procedure called a cerclage that is designed to help prevent preterm deliveries. Shortly after this procedure, she was admitted to the hospital so that she could be monitored more closely. Again, this is something that is not unusual for a triplet pregnancy, so we had no reason to be concerned. Most triplet pregnancies are considered high risk, and since this was our first pregnancy, her doctor wasn't taking any chances. We anticipated her staying in the hospital for a few months so I usually tried to spend a few nights a week at the hospital and then spend the rest of the time at home. On one particular day (a Saturday), I woke up early and, since Renita seemed to be doing fine, I went home a few hours earlier to take a nap and a shower, grab some clothes and to complete a few tasks on the "honey-do list" that Renita left for me to do to prepare for three children coming home. I planned to go back to the hospital that night but really wasn't in any particular hurry. She seemed to be doing fine, and besides, we still had three months to go until her due date.

Later that afternoon, I finished clearing out what was to become the nursery room and was on my way back to the hospital. At the time, smart phones hadn't yet been invented, so I carried a pager and an ordinary cell phone in order to be reachable in an emergency. When I was about five minutes away, my pager went off. I looked down and saw "911" followed by Renita's number at the hospital. I raced to the hospital as quickly as I could. I didn't know it at the time, but my wife's placenta had ruptured, and she was now fighting for her life. She was whisked into emergency surgery so that the doctors could perform an emergency C-section to try to save her life and the lives of our unborn children. I arrived on her floor to complete chaos. The nurses quickly told me what happened and pointed me to where I should go. I arrived in the labor and delivery surgical suite just in time to see her doctor go in and to get a glimpse of my Renita lying unconscious and being prepped for surgery. Over the next few minutes, I saw three isolettes with my very tiny brand new babies being wheeled out of the operating room headed down the hall to the neonatal intensive care unit (NICU). Richard James (RJ), Jamie, and Julia were now in a fight for their lives.

CHAPTER 3
JOY TO SORROW

For the next few minutes, I ran between the NICU and the surgical area trying to find out what was going on. I must have looked like a train wreck because one of the NICU nurses talked to me in a nice calm voice and told me to calm down and go back to the surgical waiting area for news about my wife. She said they knew who I was and where I would be and would come get me if there was a need. I went back to the waiting room and called both sets of our parents and a few close friends to share the news. Our parents were now grandparents, but Renita and the kids were still very much in danger. I promised that I would pass along any additional updates as soon as I could.

Since none of our family lived close to Cincinnati, I thought that I would be facing this crisis alone. The hospital staff was very nice and even called in a priest to stay with me and to pray while I waited. I think God knew that I needed a friend because about halfway into the procedure, in walked my pastor from our church. Renita and I had been members of his congregation for about four years and even though Pastor Freddie Piphus and I had come to know each other over the past few years, the church had a rather large congregation, so his presence was a surprise. I can't remember what we talked about in the waiting room, but I do remember my pastor being a friend when I really needed one. It seemed like we had just started talking when I saw Renita's doctor come into the waiting room. She came over to where we were seated and told me that Renita had survived the surgery and there was a good chance that she would make a total recovery. After the doctor left, Pastor Piphus and I went into the recovery room for a very short visit where I could see Renita, tell her that I loved her, and have pastor pray for us and our new children. I shared with her the good news about being a mom to three new babies, but she was so groggy that the only thing she did was grunt in response. I guess the joy of parenthood would have to wait until later.

While I was grateful that she was on the mend, I was now alone in making medical decisions for our new children, and I must admit it was a bit overwhelming. Some of the questions were easy (like if Renita had a medical emergency, should they try to revive her? I told the doctor that if she didn't, I would break her leg.) Others were harder (for example, if any of my children were to pass away, did I want to donate their body to science. I couldn't even answer that question so they saved it for later). The reality was that all three children were born weighing around 1 pound and six ounces, and the survival rate for babies born at this stage of the pregnancy was not good. Renita had recovered enough to be taken back to her room, but she was still in and out of consciousness so I didn't share this rosy prognosis with her. I just kept shuttling between her room and the NICU to check on our children. Needless to say, this was shaping up to be a busy night.

Discerning God's Purpose

CHAPTER 3

After more caffeine than the law should allow, an endless circuit of shuttling between two floors to check on four patients, and numerous phone calls to update family and friends, my body couldn't take it anymore and said *enough*. Early the next morning, I finally sat down in one of those fold-out hospital chairs and drifted off to sleep. It seems as though I had just closed my eyes when I heard a strange voice in my ear. I thought it was a dream until I felt someone shake me and say, "Mr. Kennedy, Mr. Kennedy, wake up." When I opened my eyes and remembered where I was, one of the labor and delivery nurses gave me a cup of coffee and told me that the NICU called and asked that I get up there right away. I was up and moving in an instant. I felt like I was drunk because I kept bumping into things on the way to the elevator. The NICU was only two floors up and after taking a few sips of that coffee I was ready to go.

The NICU is a secure and sterile environment, so it isn't an area that I could just rush into. It usually takes about five minutes to scrub up and get rid of any germs that could infect the infants. When I finished and finally walked into the NICU, I could see a crowd around my son's isolette. I stopped in my tracks. A nurse was performing CPR on RJ while the doctor came over to explain what happened. In the twenty-fourth week of pregnancy, many parts of the human body are not yet fully developed. When a child is born prematurely, they are forced to use organs and tissues that are often still very fragile. In my son's case, his lungs simply couldn't take the stress of having to provide oxygen to his little body and blew out. At his small size, there was no possibility for a lung transplant nor was there any other technology available that could breathe for him in order to allow the lungs to heal. The doctor said that there was literally nothing else that they could do. He kept talking, but I didn't hear anything else that he said. I was trying to comprehend the fact that my son was going to die within the next few minutes.

I was in my own world when he touched my arm and asked, "what do you want me to do?" *Huh?* He said "Do I have your permission to stop CPR?" All I could think of was the look on Renita's face if she only got to meet her son for the first time after he was already dead. I couldn't do that to her. "No," I said. "I have to get my wife." I told the doctor to keep doing what he was doing while I went up to get my wife. It might only be for a few minutes, but she was going to meet her son while he was still alive.

I ran out of the NICU and caught the elevator back down to the floor where Renita was staying. On the way to her room, I stopped by the nurses' station to grab a wheelchair and asked one of the nurses to help me get her up to the NICU. Renita was still dozing a bit so I had to wake her up and tell her what was going on. In a matter of thirty seconds, I had to have the hardest conversation that I ever had in my life. I didn't have time to sugarcoat things, so I had to tell it to her straight. I can't express the feelings that I had in trying to tell this new mother that her son was about to die. The look on her face was one of horror and disbelief. There was no time for tears because right after I told her, a nurse entered the room to help me get her out of bed and into the wheelchair. Renita was still very sore and screamed in pain while we got her

Discerning God's Purpose

CHAPTER 3

into that chair. We raced back to the elevator, got up to the NICU, scrubbed up, and went in to see our son. The doctor told her the same thing and then asked if we were ready for them to stop CPR. With tears on her cheeks, she rubbed his little body, kissed him on his forehead, prayed for a few seconds, and then invited me to do the same. When I finished, she looked at me, then looked at the doctor and told him to go ahead. The doctor looked over and signaled the nurse to stop. Immediately after she stopped, we heard the famous flat line tone coming from the monitors and realized that he was gone.

For RJ, death came very sudden, and it was over very quickly. He was here one second and gone the next. They turned off the monitors and we heard the doctor give the nurse the time. Renita let out a loud cry, and all I could do was stand still and look at his face. I still couldn't believe that he was gone. All through the night, I kept praying and believing for a miracle. During the early morning hours, when all three kids started to stabilize, I had hope that all of my children would make it. I allowed myself to think about the good times that we would have. Now, standing in front of that isolette, I realized that it was not to be. The medical team allowed us to go into a private room and spend some private time with our son before taking him away. Looking at his lifeless body, we were grateful that in the end he didn't suffer very much. If he had to go, we were glad that it happened quickly. We didn't want to let him go, but after talking to him and praying over him for a few minutes, we both realized that it was time. We handed his body over to the nurse, and she covered his face and walked out the door.

Even though we only had him for a few hours, a part of our hearts walked out of that room with him. It was hard to say goodbye.

After the nurse left with RJ, I kissed my wife and then stepped away for a few minutes to make two very important phone calls. Both sets of our parents were on their way to Cincinnati to see their new grandchildren, and now, I had the unpleasant task of telling them that there would be one less for them to see. I called my parents first. They were in the mountains of West Virginia on a busy stretch of road driving and could barely hear me. When I was in the middle of telling them the news, they hit a dead spot in cell coverage and we got cut off. By the time I was able to reconnect, they had pulled over to the side of the road and that is where I gave them the news. After taking a few minutes to absorb what I had just told them, they said that they were getting back on the road and would be there as quickly as they could. Next, I called my in-laws. They hadn't left home yet so I was able to have a longer conversation with them. I assured them that Renita was okay and that the other children were fighting but still holding their own. They told me that they would get on the road and would be there the next day. In the midst of my sorrow, I was glad to have a great relationship with both sets of our parents. They would serve as a source of strength for what was to come.

My parents arrived late that afternoon and came directly to the hospital to see how we were doing. When they walked in, all I remember was falling into my dad's arms. Besides my wife, there is no one that I am closer to than my parents. As soon as saw them, I knew that I no longer needed to shoulder this burden by myself.

Discerning God's Purpose

CHAPTER 3

Renita was still recovering from surgery, so I tried to stay strong, ease her burden, and help her through her grief. Now, with my parents there, I could finally release my own. I stood there and cried like a baby. My dad comforted me like I was a little kid again. He did his best to reassure me and kept saying everything would be OK. When I finally got myself back together, my parents made it clear that they wanted to see their new grandchildren—including their grandson.

After scrubbing up and going into the NICU, I took them to the same room where we were before so that they could meet their grandson. After the nurse brought RJ in, I remember my parents telling me how handsome he was and looking on him with pride. Of course there were tears shed, but they too said that if RJ had to die, they were glad that it happened quickly. When the nurse came back to take RJ, my parents were ready to meet their new granddaughters. I braced them for what they were about to see. A NICU is not a place where babies are lined up beside of one another as seen on TV. Each NICU child has its own "pod" with an isolette, monitors, medical equipment, and a chair for parents to use while visiting. With monitors constantly going off and doctors and nurses always buzzing around, it can be a noisy and scary place. When they visited each station, they marveled at how tiny Jamie and Julia were (they were both only eleven inches long). With all of the tubes, leads, and monitors that were going into each child, I could tell that both of my parents were starting to feel overwhelmed. We only stayed for a few minutes and then headed back down to my wife's room. My mom stayed with Renita while

I took my dad back to our house so that he could drop off their bags and start to get settled. In the meantime, I grabbed a few things and headed back to the hospital. My mom and I exchanged places so that they could go back to our house to recover from the long drive. They said that they would take care of things at home for us, and after Renita's parents arrived, they would lead them back over to the hospital. Because of my schedule for the previous few weeks, the house was not in tip-top shape and ready for guests. My parents were tired from their own trip but, without my asking, they cleaned the house from top to bottom and had my in-laws' room ready by the time they arrived. The next day, they led Renita's parents to the hospital and helped me prepare them for what they would soon see. We went through the same steps as we did the day before with them meeting RJ first and then Jamie and Julia. Both sets of parents came in and were eager to help with whatever we needed. I can only say that during our hour of need, I could not have asked for anything more. The words "thank you" never seems like it is enough for what they did that day.

Over the next few days, we made arrangements to have a memorial service at the hospital for RJ, while at the same time, constantly checking on Jamie and Julia. We had a small service for RJ at the chapel in the hospital. Only both sets of parents, and a few of the nurses who took care of RJ, and Renita and I attended. We conducted the service ourselves with a reading of the Lord's prayer and a few words from each member of our family on RJ's impact on our lives during his short stay with us. The service was over in less than thirty minutes, and afterwards, a representative

Discerning God's Purpose

CHAPTER 3

from the funeral home came to pick up RJ's body. Because RJ's death was so unexpected, we made the decision to cremate RJ. One of Renita's sorority sisters happened to work at a funeral home and helped us get through this painful process. After everything was complete, we were given an urn about the same size as a large egg that contained his ashes. We made the decision to keep his ashes and to bury them with whichever one of us (Renita or I) died first. With this painful task completed, we focused our efforts on keeping Jamie and Julia alive.

Both Jamie and Julia were still in very critical condition but Jamie's situation started to become alarming. She started to develop a number of complications but the biggest concern was her kidneys not functioning like they should. The same doctor who was with us when RJ passed away came over to tell us all that was going on with Jamie. He told us that there was a very real possibility that we could lose her if the situation didn't change. By this time, I was starting to get upset. I began to think of this man as the grim reaper because every time he came around he only delivered bad news. I wanted him to stay as far away from my children as possible and wasn't shy in telling him so. It was an unfair accusation, one that I later apologized for, but it reflected my feelings at the time. For one of the few times in my life, I felt absolutely powerless. My child was fighting for her life and there was nothing that I could do to make her better. I remember getting angry with God and saying, "What else can go wrong." Soon we would find out.

I remember hearing stories about people who do everything wrong during a pregnancy but still are blessed to deliver healthy babies. Here we were trying to do everything "right," yet here we were. We had already lost one child and were about to lose another. Even worse, our youngest daughter, Julia, had developed a significant brain bleed, and doctors were now unsure if she would live. It just wasn't fair. After my confrontation with the doctor, he began to think of himself as bad luck so he asked one of his associates to take over with Julia. The new doctor decided to take different approach. She still told us what was going on and was realistic about Julia's prognosis, but she was cautiously optimistic and gave us reason for hope. She ended the conversation by saying "If you believed in God, now would be a good time to pray." She knew that Jamie and Julia faced a tough road ahead but that with God, all things were possible. My faith was surely being tested at the time, but nevertheless, I still prayed and also asked others to keep us in their prayers.

The next day, shortly after I had finished praying over Julia, I looked around and saw my pastor entering the NICU. Since seeing him on the day of delivery, I hadn't had a chance to call him or anyone else at the church so I was very surprised to see him walk into the NICU. I took him to the pods and introduced him to our two children, and he prayed for their wellbeing. Afterwards, we visited in the waiting room for a few minutes so that he could pray for Renita and me as well. He told me to call him if I needed anything and then he was on his way. After he left, I began to think that maybe God hadn't forgotten about me after all. A

Discerning God's Purpose

CHAPTER 3

short time later, the grim reaper was on duty and after making his rounds, told me that Jamie's condition still hadn't improved. She still needed to pass urine and have a bowel movement in order to remove the toxins that were building up in her body. Shortly thereafter, I found myself praying one of the strangest prayers that I could think of. I prayed for Jamie to pee and poop. I remember thinking "God, if you are really up there, please help Jamie to pee and poop. I pray this prayer in the mighty name of Jesus, Amen." After I finished, I smiled thinking about what my Sunday school-teaching grandmother would think of that prayer. Well, I guess the prayer worked because the next day, when Renita, my mom, my dad, and I were visiting her pod, Jamie started to pee. We started to whoop and holler like our favorite team just won the championship game. We did this every time we saw her relieve herself and even got the nurses and other parents in on the act. What a sight we must have been.

After Jamie relieved herself, her vital signs started to improve, and while she was still in danger, we thought that she had stabilized and would soon be on the road to recovery. Julia's brain bleed had stopped so her condition began to stabilize as well. Since my parents had been with us for about a week, they thought that it was a good time to go back home, wash clothes, check on things around their house, and then return to Cincinnati in about a week. Both sets of parents saw that there was a long, hard road ahead, so they had decided to take turns staying with us until Jamie and Julia were out of danger. Renita's parents stayed on and took care of things at home while we largely remained at the hospital. A few days later, Renita was well enough and was released. We didn't want to leave and even offered to pay to stay in the hospital room so that we could remain close to the NICU around the clock; however, there was a shortage of beds and the hospital needed the space. I remember taking Renita home and upon entering our house, consoling her as she let out the most blood-curdling scream that I had ever heard. We anticipated bringing all three kids home from the hospital, and with what had transpired over the last week that was not to be.

With Renita now home from the hospital, we developed a new routine. She was still moving gingerly and trying to recover from surgery so I elected to extend my paternity leave for a bit longer. Since I wasn't working, we would wake up early and head to the hospital so that we could talk to the doctors and residents during their rounds. After getting an update, we would stay for the rest of the day. Since the nurses worked twelve- hour shifts from seven until seven (day and night), we would stay to find out who the nurses were for our children, and make sure that everything was okay before leaving to go home just after nine P.M. After we arrived home, we would call the NICU every few hours to check on our children then try to get a few hours' sleep. Then the next morning, we would do it all over again.

Sometimes in the midst of trouble, you have to find something to laugh about to ease the stress of the day. Our first laugh came while Renita's parents were still staying with us. After living this new routine for a few days, Renita looked at me one day and said that I looked tired. I thought *no kidding*. At least she had a

Discerning God's Purpose

CHAPTER 3

few days to get a little rest, but I had been on this particular treadmill since the day that all three were born (I know, the thought was wrong but hey, at this point, I hadn't had a lot of sleep in over a week so give me some slack). She asked her parents to take us to the hospital that day. Normally, I would say that I am OK and just keep going but since I was feeling tired and wanted to keep us safe, I decided to accept the help. Boy, was that a dumb decision. Everything was fine that morning as her dad drove to the hospital and dropped us off with no problem. When it came time to leave, things got a little dicey. Renita's dad grew up in the country. At the time, he and my mother-in-law lived in Richmond, Virginia, and while it is the "Capital of the Confederacy," it still has a small-town feel. Driving is bit different in Cincinnati as people tend not to be as forgiving. It was dark when we left, and in his defense, Mr. Richardson wasn't familiar with the traffic flow. The way that we needed to drive home involved coming down a hill and making a sharp right turn that was almost 180 degrees in order to get on the highway to go home. Right before the turn, there is a stoplight that allows a right turn on red after stopping, but the trick is to do it fast because the oncoming traffic doesn't slow down. Well, on this particular night, it was overcast, and my father-in-law had trouble seeing beyond the turn. After stopping for the red light, he made a wide slow turn just as the oncoming traffic started to approach. Seeing the cars getting closer, my life started to flash before my eyes. With the cars getting closer and the drivers honking their horns, my father-in-law yelled to no one in particular "you know which way I'm trying to go" and continued his turn. I thought for sure that we were getting ready to be T-boned and that very soon, I would be seeing St. Peter at the pearly gates. I was almost on my knees in the front seat praying that the other drivers would have mercy on us and wouldn't hit the car. Fortunately, no one hit us, and we made it the rest of the way home without incident. That night when we were alone, I told Renita that was the last time that I would be riding with her father. It's been seventeen years since that happened, and we still laugh about it to this day—but never again did I step into a car with my father-in-law behind the wheel.

A few days later, Renita and I began to think that the worst was over. Jamie had stabilized and looked to be improving. She started to have output on a regular basis, and the lab reports looked encouraging. On Sunday evening after a full day at the hospital, we went home to rest after the nurse assured us that there had been no change in her condition and that she was still stable. After we got home, we still called the NICU every few hours to make sure that everything was still OK. We climbed into bed and dropped off for a few hours of sleep. I woke up around four in the morning and called the nurses' station to check on Jamie and Julia. Jamie's nurse sounded like she was out of breath when she came on the line. She told me that they were just about to call us because Jamie's vital signs had dropped, and they had called in the neonatologist. I hung up the phone, jumped out of bed and told Renita to get dressed.

"Jamie's in trouble," I said. Renita was still a little sore from the surgery, but the news of Jamie's distress kicked her adrenaline into high gear. We got dressed quickly, briefly told my in-laws

Discerning God's Purpose

CHAPTER 3

what was going on, and headed to the hospital. When we arrived in the NICU, the neonatologist met us by Jamie's pod and told us that the toxins in her body just became too much for her. She had fought so hard that her body was simply giving out. She was still alive but would not survive for much longer. There was nothing more that they could do. This time, there was no team of doctors and nurses performing CPR, only Jamie's nurse and the doctor. She was still alive but was fading fast. The nurse opened up the isolette and we began to pray over her. So that we wouldn't upset the other families in the NICU, we went to a side room so that we could have our final few moments with Jamie in private. She was still hooked up to all kinds of monitors, but we were at least able to hold our baby. Since Jamie had been so sick, we had only been able to touch her while she was laying in the isolate, but even then we had to have on gloves and a mask. Now, in her final moments, we were able to hold her in our arms. When it was clear that death was near, we asked that all of the tubes be removed and that only her main monitor remain. We took turns holding our baby, telling her that we loved her and that it was okay for her to join her brother in heaven. I was holding Jamie a few minutes later when she peacefully passed away. Two babies in ten days.

In much the same way as we did for RJ, we held Jamie for a few more minutes, prayed over her, and then let the nurse take her away. As it turned out, we didn't have much time to grieve. Just after Jamie passed, Julia's night nurse came over and told us that Julia's vital signs were all over the place. Since she was also in grave condition, we began to fear the worst. That is when we met a person who was to become our bedrock during Julia's stay. Her name was Nurse Pat, and she was assigned as Julia's new nurse for the day. Nurse Pat had been at that hospital and working in the NICU for over thirty years and immediately made a connection with us. She calmed us down and told us that in the case of multiples, when one sibling dies, the vital signs of the remaining sibling tend to fluctuate quite wildly. It was, she explained, Julia's way of grieving for her sister. She said that the same thing happened on the day that RJ passed. We were just so emotionally spent with RJ that they either hadn't told us or we failed to recognize what was going on. Nurse Pat also told us that Julia was quite a little fighter and this trait would serve her well on her road to recovery. In the midst of our darkest hour, here was a person who was giving us hope. God still provides.

Discerning God's Purpose

CHAPTER 4
HOPE

Over the course of ten days, our lives had turned upside down. This was not what I had in mind when Renita's doctor told us that we were pregnant some six months before. We now found ourselves planning a second memorial service and making arrangements to cremate another child. My parents came back to town, and this time, three of my aunts came in as well. We held a small memorial service in the hospital chapel that was similar to the one we had for RJ, but this time, we had more people in attendance. We asked family members and friends to participate in the service by reading the Lord's Prayer, the Twenty-Third psalm and allowing a moment for anyone to say whatever was on their heart. Several of our friends attended and even Pastor Piphus showed up unannounced and sat in the audience just as a sign of support. Again, just like RJ, we made the decision to cremate Jamie with the new understanding that each of us would be buried with the ashes of one child. We were more than a little ticked off when the representative from the funeral home showed up at the end of the service with a small box with which to carry Jamie's remains. We were not going to allow Jamie to be carried out of the hospital in a box that was originally used for office supplies. We wrapped Jamie up in a small hospital blanket and carried her through the back corridors of the hospital and out the back entrance to the waiting funeral home van. Only then did we hand her to that funeral home representative. He may have still placed Jamie in that box, but at least she didn't endure that indignity when I had something to say about it.

After the service, everyone took turns going in to the NICU and praying over Julia. For the next few days, family members continued to visit Julia, but inevitably they had to start making their way home.

For the first time since delivery, Renita and I now found ourselves at home alone. That's when our friends stepped in and offered to help. Suddenly, people started stopping by the house or the hospital just to see how we were doing. Longtime friends from out of town started flying in just to check on us. I'll never forget one of Renita's friends who just had a baby herself, dropped everything to fly in and be with us. That lady (and you know who you are) cemented herself in our lives forever and has since become the sister that Renita never had. We will always be grateful to everyone who helped us in our time of need, but we were and are grateful to this person in particular. There is a saying that the Lord may not come when you want Him, but He'll always be right on time. In our case, truer words were never spoken.

After Jamie's memorial service, Julia started to show signs of improvement. I was wary because the same thing happened with Jamie before she took a turn of the worse; however, this time her condition continued to stabilize. Her brain bleed had resolved and

Discerning God's Purpose

CHAPTER 4

they were able to start treatment on some of her other issues (like jaundice). Jaundice occurs when there is a build-up of a naturally occurring substance in the blood called bilirubin. The normal treatment is something called phototherapy in which the child is surrounded with a special light in order to reduce the levels of bilirubin in the body. I had to laugh when they put sunglasses on Julia and put her in something that looked like a tanning booth. At least we found another reason to smile.

Over the next few weeks, her condition gradually improved. She went from grave, to critical, to serious and finally to fair condition. She spent the Christmas holiday in the NICU, and we spent a fairly long night with her on New Year's Eve. People feared that the change from one century to another would cause all sorts of problems with the country's technology infrastructure. To make sure critical places like hospitals were safe, emergency manual systems were at the ready, just in case. In the NICU, hand-pump-operated oxygen containers and extra people were standing by in case the extra personnel were needed. After the New Year, Julia's condition continued to improve to the point to where, toward the end of January, the medical staff finally started talking about her going home. The nurses started giving her oxygen tests (having her breathe room air instead of oxygen), car seat tests (placing her in a car seat while she was still hooked up to monitors to make sure her oxygen, heart, and other critical functions would remain stable), and all of the other checks that are standard before a baby leaves the NICU to go home. Also, in the days leading up to her release, she underwent the normal hospital baby checks for wellness. That's when we found out that Julia was deaf and had a developmental disability that would later be diagnosed as cerebral palsy.

As you can well imagine, Julia's diagnosis was not a part of my life's plan. Before we got pregnant, Renita and I were focused on our careers. We had things all mapped out. Now, we were focused on Julia and doing everything that we could to keep her well. While I was happy that Julia would soon be coming home, I still was angry and had a bone to pick with God—and I let Him know it.

Discerning God's Purpose

CHAPTER 5
ESTABLISHING A RELATIONSHIP WITH GOD

When I was a child, I was raised and baptized in the Catholic Church. I was not a deeply religious person, but as the saying goes, I had a drug problem. My parents drug me to church. I went to service, got baptized when I was nine, and even served as an altar boy, but like a lot of kids, I really didn't have much of a relationship with God. When I graduated from high school and went off to college, I didn't attend church on a regular basis. I still believed in God, but other things got in the way (like parties, studying, and sleep).

After college, I went to work; first in the military and then as a consultant. I met my future wife while I was still in the military. Renita and I were introduced by a mutual friend right before I left for six months of training at a new duty station. Since I was leaving within the next few days, we didn't have a chance to begin our relationship in a traditional way. Instead of going to dinner or a movie, we got to know each other over the phone. For six months, we talked for an hour or so every Saturday morning. In the middle of my assignment, I came home for two weeks while on leave so we had the opportunity to go out on a formal date. Since we lived three hours from one another, we decided to go out on a double date with our mutual friend and her beau. Our friend lived near Renita and offered to drive her to our date. Everything was going fine until our friend had a sudden change of plans. Since Renita was now stranded, I offered to drive her. It was technically still our first date, and Renita only knew me from the series of phone calls that we had over the past few months. While she agreed to let me take her home, she still warned of the dire consequences that I would face from her extended family if I decided to do anything unsavory. The trip went fine and soon I returned to my training assignment and our weekly phone calls. During our calls, one of the things that we discussed was our faith. I still identified myself as Catholic while she was raised as Baptist. At the time, I still wasn't a regular attendee at church but tried to do a little better when she was around (do what you have to do to impress a girl).

When we decided to get married, we agreed to attend premarital counseling out of respect for my upbringing in the Catholic Church. We got married at her home church with three ministers officiating (the pastor that she grew up with, the current pastor of the church, and a Catholic priest). As a newlywed couple, we made an effort to find a church that would serve both of our needs. I still didn't feel a close connection with God but wanted to make my wife happy. Outside of my Catholic upbringing, I only had two points of reference with other preachers. The first was listening to stories of how my grandparents or other extended family members of different faiths would invite their pastor over once a year for a chicken dinner; the second was hearing these same family members complain about how the pastors were living high

Discerning God's Purpose

CHAPTER 5

on the hog while their members struggled to pay tithes and make ends meet. Needless to say, I didn't have a real positive view of these preachers; therefore I didn't really see a need for a close and personal relationship with the Lord Almighty.

Early in our marriage, we moved around quite a bit so Renita was always on the lookout for a church that had good music, good teaching and where we would feel welcome. Out of respect for me, Renita tried attending a few Catholic services with me but found the services to be boring and she really didn't get a whole lot out of the message. Over the next few years, we also tried a few other churches but never found one that we both connected with. One time, we even attended a church where the pastor called out a few members to make an extra effort toward giving. I remember this dude telling one man "You're an attorney. You can give more than that." I was appalled. At another church, I heard some backwoods preacher working himself into a tizzy with a bunch of hollering and screaming along with dire warnings about what would happen if "Y'all don't get right with God." I started to lose hope of even finding God in some of these houses of "worship." If these jokers were accurately describing who God was (a mean or a jealous God), I very much wanted to keep God at a distance.

Things started to change about five years into our marriage when we moved to Cincinnati to accept new jobs. Again, Renita wanted to look for a church that would serve our needs, and I went along to make her happy. We heard about this church with a dynamic young preacher and decided to check it out. We walked in and the atmosphere was inviting. The music was great (the minister of music was a professional musician so he recruited people who could actually sing) and the pastor had a heart for teaching. He would reference different scriptures in the Bible and then show how they provided guidance for everyday life. He didn't come across as the second coming of Jesus Christ but as a person who makes mistakes and just like the rest of us, tried to be a better person every day. I was even motivated to go out and buy a study Bible so that I could follow along with his preaching. After a few months, I got the opportunity to get to know the pastor, and we would occasionally schedule time to have lunch and generally just talk about life. He knew that I had a business background so he asked me for suggestions on how to improve the business operations of the church. In time, he started to talk to me about faith on a level that I never experienced before. He didn't talk about a mean God or a jealous God, but one who loved me and wanted to have a close and personal relationship with me. One time, I remember wondering why God wanted a relationship with me. That night, I remember having a dream unlike any before. An image surrounded by fire looked at me and simply said, "Read the Bible." I remember waking up and thinking that maybe there was something to this relationship stuff after all. I didn't know where it would lead, but I knew that somewhere, someone was trying to communicate with me.

 I started getting involved in different activities at the church. I got to know some of the men in the church and was even invited to join the men's choir. Renita thought this was hilarious (me the reluctant churchgoer was now in the choir). I will never be confused with being a great singer. The best way to describe my singing is to say that if I were required to audition for the true church choir, I would be asked to join the security ministry instead. The men's choir was really an excuse for a bunch of guys to get together to have a little fun while singing an occasional song. Still, I was amazed that when we did sing (usually once a month during the main service) we actually sounded good (even with me in it). My experience with the choir also served as an awakening that let me know what God was all about. Since most of the songs related to some sort of scripture, it forced me to read the Bible and in doing so, enabled me to get to know God for myself. I started with little steps such as reading a few passages here and there and then asking God to grant me some small request. Deep down, I still didn't feel the need to depend on God, but more and more, I became aware of His presence. Still, my career was rolling along fine, I was married to a woman whom I loved, nothing really bad had ever happened in my life, so as far as I was concerned, everything was great. All of that changed after the pregnancy.

In talking with Pastor as well as some of the older guys in the choir, I learned that building a relationship with God was like building a relationship with any other friend. Sometimes, you needed to be brutally honest in communicating your feelings. After RJ and Jamie died, I let Him have it. I asked God how could He say that He loved me and still let this happen. What did I do to deserve to suffer like this? How could He be so cruel to let little children suffer like this? On and on I went, blaming God for what happened to our family and holding Him responsible for the pain that it caused. I wasn't the only one who was upset. My wife had her own issues with God. She kept asking "Why has God forsaken us?" We felt that God was somehow paying us back for something we or some ancestor did that made God angry. I knew that I wasn't perfect, but I knew I didn't do anything to deserve this.

Admittedly, I was in a funk. After RJ and Jamie died, I didn't want to have anything to do with God. I stopped going to church and just focused all of my efforts on healing and protecting Renita and Julia. I wasn't mean to people that I knew from church, but I wasn't exactly welcoming either. I guess some folks got offended because we started receiving fewer and fewer phone calls to check up and see how we were doing. It didn't bother me. I thought if this is how God wants things, then so be it. Things changed one day when one of my friends who also was a deacon called and asked if he and a few other deacons that I knew from the men's choir could stop by to see how we were doing. He was one of my friends so I said OK. At the time, I felt the need to be around other men, and while I had a close relationship with my own father, my parents lived over five hundred miles away so I didn't see them on a regular basis. Truth be told, the best time for me when I was active in church was actually after choir rehearsals were over. Many times we would gather in small groups and just talk. Many of the men were older and didn't want anything other than friendly conversation and the chance to help if needed. Now, they wanted to come over just to see how we were doing. Maybe God wasn't mad at me after all.

Discerning God's Purpose

CHAPTER 5

When they came over, I was glad to see them. Many of them were much older than I, and in a way, served as father figures with my own father being hundreds of miles away. These men knew that I needed an emotional lift so they rallied in my time of need. They came by the house to offer communion and a few words of encouragement. I couldn't be mad at them. Some even took the time to drop by the NICU to show their support and in general help me pass the time. During these tough times, these men of faith were willing to share their own stories, some being fairly close to what I was going through, and the role that faith had in getting through it. Other times, they would only say that even in the bad times, God was still with me. They would say that they didn't know how, but in some way, God would take this experience and turn it into something good. Initially I was reluctant to receive their words of wisdom, but over time, I was grateful for the support.

While I had the men's support group from church, my wife had her own support system which consisted of church friends, neighbors, her sorority sisters as well as a few very close lifelong friends. When tragedy struck, they were right there. They made food for us when we were doing our shuttle runs to the hospital; checked on her throughout the day to see how she was doing; and some came by the NICU to visit Julia and to show love to Renita in her time of need. They shared with her some of the same messages that the guys were sharing with me. One of her closest friends said that RJ and Jamie had fulfilled their mission on earth and were now Julia's guardian angels. Their assignment had been to get her here safely, and then to go up and watch over her from heaven.

She even said God must have something special planned for Julia because He sent two angels to make sure that she was alright.

Gradually, I began to think that maybe God really hadn't forsaken us after all. We started noticing little words of encouragement in our everyday lives. I passed by a quote that said "sorrow endures for a night, but joy is coming in the morning." Another time, a friend reminded Renita that she "couldn't have a beautiful rainbow without rain." After a few weeks of paternity leave, I went back to work. Since Renita was still on leave, she would go to the hospital during the day, and I would relieve her when I finished work and stay late into the evening. Many times, I would be the only parent left. When I needed a break, I would have the waiting area all to myself. It was during those times that I once again began having conversations with God. Julia was stable so there was nothing else to do but to talk to Him. At first my conversations were still full of anger, but gradually I would just ask for guidance on what to do. I was honest with Him about my pain but I also thanked Him for the words of encouragement that He sent my way. Since Renita and I would soon be responsible for taking care of this child, I admitted that I was in unfamiliar territory and asked for help. I once heard someone say that you meet God during good times but you really don't get to know Him until the tough times. That certainly was true for me. It was during those times at the hospital where I felt Him say that I was never alone. He said that He had a plan for me but that I had to learn how to rely on Him. Growing up, I had been taught to depend on myself. Now, God was telling me to depend on Him. I learned that even

Discerning God's Purpose

CHAPTER 5

great leaders need to be led. I also learned that God never does anything or causes something to happen without planning for a greater purpose.

Suddenly, my dream that told me to read the Bible started to make sense. God wanted to tell me something. I didn't start by trying to read it cover to cover but just looked for topics that suited me. I became interested in the story of Job and how he lost everything including his business, his family, and his health only to have God not only restore what he lost but to give him double what he had before (Now I know the meaning "double for your trouble"). I read the story of Joseph and how he was betrayed by his own family and sold into slavery only to rise to become the second most powerful man in Egypt. Another story that I read was about Moses and how he led the Israelites out of Egypt. Moses was born into the family of Egyptian slaves and had a severe speech problem, yet God still chose him to lead His people. These stories served as a source of inspiration for me. It was God's way of telling me that God didn't call the equipped, He equipped the called. It was God's way of telling me that I had everything that I needed to care for Julia. He had me in the palm of His hand and I wasn't going to fail.

These stories reminded me of my own life and how many situations could have ended in tragedy but for the presence of God. When I was seventeen, a friend and I were driving on a rainy night on a busy highway when suddenly I lost control of the vehicle. I spun out, crossed four lanes of heavy traffic, and came to a stop on the far side of the road. I had a minor fender bender but was otherwise unhurt. There had also been times when I was down on my luck financially when suddenly I would either receive a financial blessing from an unexpected source or otherwise found a way to earn money and take care of my family. By reading these Bible stories and having nighttime conversations with God, I realized that there was only one way that I survived and that was through the grace and mercy of Almighty God. I realized that I had no choice. I had to depend on Him.

In 2 Timothy 4:7, when he knows that he is about to die, Paul says, "I have fought the good fight. I have finished the race. I have served the Lord faithfully." When you fulfill your purpose, many people have a revelation that the end is near. I had no such revelation. On the contrary, I felt that Julia survived for a reason. She had a purpose to fulfill. I also knew that it was no accident that Renita and I were her parents. God chose us for this assignment of raising Julia. Not only that, but in the years to come, I would also see God's hand of restoration. That would come later. For now, I had an assignment, and it was one that I planned to do my best to fulfill.

Discerning God's Purpose

UNDERSTANDING MY PURPOSE

We consider Julia to be our miracle baby. Recent advancements in medical technology have improved a premature baby's chances of survival but, according to an article published by BMJ.com (formerly known as the British Medical Journal), the survival rate in 1999 (her birth year) for a baby born at 24 weeks gestation and weighing just 624 grams (approximately 1 pound 6 ounces) was between 9 and 21 percent. Throw in the fact that she was part of a multiple-birth scenario, and the survival rate declines even further. Yet, in spite of the odds, she survived. I know of only one reason for her miraculous survival—God. We know that He has a special assignment in mind for her. My job is not to figure out that assignment but to prepare her for whatever He has in mind.

I'll be honest, when we found out about the challenges that Julia faced, I was scared. At the time, we didn't know of nor had ever interacted with anyone who was deaf. In addition, we only knew of a few people in our family who had developmental disabilities and we only saw them on rare occasions (in years past, people tended to "hide" those in their families who had disabilities or just labeled them as "slow"). If God truly had special plans for Julia, we knew that we were going to need help. In the hospital,

God revealed that the only thing that I could truly count on in this world was Him and His word. Based on that, I was sure of two things going forward: First, God didn't bring us this far to simply leave us or forsake us. Second, God would provide us with whatever we needed in order to complete our assignment. I wasn't sure of what we were in store for but I knew that we were not alone. We had a challenging assignment but fortunately, God sent some very special people across our path to help us figure it all out.

CHAPTER 6
GOING HOME

After three months in the NICU, we were finally able to take Julia home. I probably was more careful driving on that trip than at any time before or since. After getting home, Renita and I went through what I like to call NICU withdrawal. There were no doctors or nurses around as a safety net to diagnose the slightest abnormality so we had to figure out things for ourselves. We were almost afraid to touch Julia for fear that she would somehow get sick. We had her first pediatric appointment scheduled within the next few days so we tried to relax and enjoy some quality time with our new baby. Unfortunately, we didn't even make it to her first appointment before facing our first challenge. The day after we got her home, I had to run to the office to pick up a few things while Renita stayed home with Julia. No sooner had I arrived when my cell phone rang. It was Renita saying that she had just called 911 because Julia wasn't breathing. She explained that she just finished feeding Julia when she noticed her face starting to turn blue. Luckily, we didn't live far from the nearest fire station so they were there in no time. Also, we stopped by the station a few days before to let them know that a deaf child would be in the

CHAPTER 6

neighborhood. When they got the call, they were pulling up to the house less than three minutes later.

When the paramedics showed up, Renita let them in quickly so that they could see what was going on. They started checking for a blocked airway or anything else that would cause Julia to stop breathing. That's when it happened. They heard a squirting sound followed by a smell that told them that Julia had just filled her diaper. She was straining so hard to relieve herself that her face turned blue. After she emptied out, her face returned to normal. The paramedics started erupting in laughter. They told Renita that Julia would be fine but to be on the safe side, they would take her to the hospital so that the doctors could check her out. Since we had just left Good Samaritan a few days before and the staff was familiar with her, Renita asked that Julia be taken there. Also, my office was very close to the hospital so I told Renita that I would just meet them there. The doctors at Good Samaritan checked her out and said that Julia was just fine but decided to keep her overnight for observation. We spent an uneventful night at the hospital and returned home the next day.

The next morning, we had another challenge. Julia came home from the hospital while still on oxygen. She only needed a minimal amount, and the doctors said she would probably only need it for another week or so until she could fully breathe on her own. Well, the day after we returned from our unexpected hospital trip, we woke up to find that her oxygen wasn't on. In our rush to go to bed the night before, I forgot to change out the oxygen tank. When we woke up that morning, the tank was empty. We started to panic. We looked at her monitors (she had a small monitor for oxygen readings), and thankfully it showed her saturation level to be above 95 percent. Since she couldn't hear, she was still sound asleep during our moment of panic. Still, we weren't sure so again we called the nurses' station. After a few quick questions, the staff said that there was nothing to worry about and just let the pediatrician examine her at her appointment that afternoon. When we took her in, the doctor checked her out and said that she was fine. Dr. Brad, her pediatrician, even laughed and told us that we simply completed her oxygen test a few days earlier than planned. He told us to go home, relax and enjoy our baby. We left out of that doctor's office with a newfound sense of relief.

When we got home, we began to realize that Julia would be OK. She was breathing on her own and by all measures was adjusting well to life at home. Over the next few months, we got used to our new normal. In addition to the normal new baby doctor appointments, we had a slew of audiology and therapy appointments. Our pediatrician kept assuring us that things were fine and that Julia was continuing to develop normally. He assured us that with a few lifestyle adjustments, there was no reason why Julia couldn't live a fairly normal life. Since this was our first pregnancy, a number of our friends and family wanted to celebrate our impending good fortune by throwing multiple baby showers. Because of early delivery, we didn't have a chance to have any celebrations before the triplets' arrival. After experiencing the tragedy of losing two children in ten days, all of the other planned celebrations were put on hold. Now that Julia was out of danger and well on the road to

CHAPTER 6

recovery, the celebrations could begin in earnest. Our friends and family threw not one but a total four baby showers in Ohio, Maryland, and Virginia. We were truly blessed with the outpouring of generosity and that allowed us to start Julia off with more clothes, bottles, and toys than she would ever need.

At the time, we were facing a significant financial challenge. A few months after we took Julia home, Renita was laid off from her job. She hadn't been able to work since before the pregnancy and when her maternity plus the additional protections granted under the Family Medical Leave Act (FMLA) were exhausted, the company let her go. After years of being a two-income household, we now had to adjust our lifestyle in order to live off of one income. Looking back, this was probably a blessing in disguise. With all of the medical and therapy appointments that Julia required at this stage of life, it would have been impossible for both of us to have full-time jobs. What turned out to be a bigger surprise came almost a year later when I was laid off. This one truly came out of nowhere, and with our focus being on Julia and her wellbeing, we tried to figure out what to do next. We had bills to pay, and I wanted to find a job so that we could continue to provide Julia with the care that she needed. As strange as it may sound, however, things worked out for the best. We both received severance packages when we were laid off so we were able to limp along in the short term and focus on Julia.

During one of the in-home therapy sessions, the occupational therapist suggested we try water therapy as a way to maximize Julia's range of motion. The idea is for a parent to get into the water and work under the direction of a therapist so that the child will stay comfortable and cooperative in a strange environment. Since I liked the water and was a fairly strong swimmer, I decided to get into the pool with Julia. During those sessions, Julia and I started to form a close bond. I knew that I would play an important role in her life and my presence was critical to preparing her for God's assignment. Not too long ago, Renita and I were clearing out some old boxes and discovered a picture of the two of us as we finished one of these therapy sessions. We both looked happy, and it captured for me the true definition of being a father—being there when she needed me the most.

Discerning God's Purpose

CHAPTER 7
SEEKING WISDOM

A person can only lead if they have the knowledge and wisdom to lead others. No one is born with wisdom, it must be learned. I remember when I was six or seven years old, I was afraid to go near the water. I didn't want to go swimming because I was afraid that I would drown. My parents didn't want me to have a lifetime fear of the water, so they enrolled me in swimming lessons. Once I learned how to swim, I grew to love the water. When I conquered my fear of swimming, I remember my Dad saying that knowledge is the key to overcoming fear. He said, "You will face many challenges in life. You better learn how to overcome those obstacles if you want to be successful." That lesson has stuck with me ever since.

When we first found out that we were pregnant, the first thing that we did was go out and buy the book *What to Expect When You're Expecting*. When Renita went on bedrest, she used her time to read that book and other materials about what we were soon going to face as new parents. After delivery, Dr. Brad would come by the NICU occasionally to check on Julia's progress. Although she was still under the care of the hospital neonatologist, he still would drop by to keep tabs on her progress in preparation for her release. As Julia got closer to her release date, his visits became more frequent. One day, I happened to see him in the NICU looking over Julia's chart. He knew that Julia was going to be released soon and could see that I was starting to get nervous. I even had a copy of one of those parenting books with me and was reading it (skimming it really) to pass the time and to pick up a few tips. After exchanging pleasantries and getting his perspective on Julia's progress, Dr. Brad decided that it was now time to give me a dose of reality. He said, "You might as well throw that book away. Julia is not going to be a typical child. She will have some unique challenges and nothing in that book is going to help you. Besides, you will only get frustrated by reading that book. Julia is going to do things on her own timetable and in her own way so don't worry yourself about arbitrary timelines." He was honest and said that Julia would probably be late in achieving most of her developmental milestones, "But that doesn't matter. The key is for her to achieve them." He told me to love her, do my best to look out for her, and let God take care of everything else. Out of all the advice that I received as a parent, I have to say that this was the best.

Whenever anyone is admitted into the hospital, the staff normally keeps a chart close by in order to keep track of their progress. The chart is updated multiple times throughout the day and is usually discussed by staff at shift change for nurses and doctor's rounds. Technology has advanced to the point that these charts are now kept in digital form, but in 1999, the charts were kept in paper format and stored in a binder at bedside. About a week into her stay, I noticed the binder and picked it up to look at

CHAPTER 7

Julia's progress. It might as well have been written in Greek. I have a degree in business, not medicine, so I didn't know about medical terminology. I would stop one of the nurses, and they were kind enough to explain what the terms meant. In order to keep abreast of what was going on, I knew that Renita and I needed to get smart about the basics of medicine and fast. We started talking to Nurse Pat and soon it seemed that we were getting a crash course in medicine. She always reminded us that we were the parents so we had a right to know and understand everything that was contained in Julia's chart. Pretty soon, we were confident enough to ask the doctors about certain aspects of her treatment. When Julia experienced her brain bleed, we asked the radiologist to show us her CT (computer tomography) scan and to describe what he was seeing. When Julia experienced jaundice, the staff explained her blood count levels and shared their strategy for treatment. We were able to ask questions and fully understand why they favored a particular course of action prior to starting treatment. Since we were rarely at the hospital at the same time, Renita and I would share everything that we learned during our individual time at the hospital so that we both had a complete picture of what was going on. By asking questions, we learned that just like anyone else, medical professionals are more than willing to share their knowledge. At the same time, our inquisitive nature served another purpose. It showed that we had a very keen interest in the welfare of our child. When parents show up and demonstrate interest, the child usually receives more attention and, in many cases, better results. Not only did we find this to be true at the hospital, but at schools later on down the road. When people see that you are watching, they will naturally pay closer attention to what they are doing and will do a better job. We had a fabulous team working with Julia and had no complaints; still, we were always watching, just in case.

As parents, Renita and I believe very strongly that parents must do everything within our power to protect and advocate for our children. In order to do this effectively, parents must have full knowledge of what's going on in their child's life. Medically speaking, not only did we need to know our child's medical history, but we needed to know why the medical professionals pursued a particular course of action. This knowledge was very important going forward because we were able to question the benefits and concerns of certain procedures instead of simply going along with whatever a doctor recommends. With us, medical professionals must be able to articulate why it was medically necessary, show data where such treatment has worked in the past, and discuss any risks associated with the recommended treatment. In short, we wanted to make sure that the recommended treatment had previously been proven effective and that Julia would not become a medical experiment. We weren't going to be buffaloed.

With Julia's unique set of circumstances, not only did we have to get smart on medical terminology, but other services as well. Before leaving the hospital, her social worker told us that because Julia was delayed developmentally, she qualified for in-home therapy services. Shortly, we were contacted by the Early Childhood Education (ECE) coordinator for our local school district to map out a plan for Julia to receive occupational and physical therapy at

CHAPTER 7

home. This was our first introduction to something known as the Individual Family Services Plan (IFSP). As stated on the website kidsneeds.com, the IFSP "documents and guides the early intervention process for children with disabilities and their families. The IFSP is the vehicle through which effective early intervention is implemented in accordance with Part C of the Individuals with Disabilities Education Act (IDEA)." This legislation was passed by the U.S. Congress in 1990 (and updated in 2004) in order to provide children with disabilities with free appropriate public education (FAPE) that is designed to meet their needs. All of this legal mumbo jumbo means that Julia was entitled to therapy at an early age in order to get ready for school. As Julia grew older and enrolled in elementary school, the IFSP is replaced by an IEP (Individual Education Plan). The concept is the same, but it covers services required to support Julia in school. We still had private therapy that focused on skills for life, but the IEP is a tool that requires schools to accommodate kids with special needs. At this point, I had never heard of the IDEA or the IEP; however, it would become a critical tool in advocating on Julia's behalf for years to come.

Growing up, my parents used to encourage me to study in school because "knowledge is power." They were not the first to come up with this statement, but they certainly went out of their way to emphasize this point to me. When it came to career choices, my parents insisted that I go to college first and then enter the workforce. It's not as if the information that I learned in college was critical over the course of my entire working career; far from it. Studies show that current information learned is usually obsolete within five years of discovery. What is critical in going to school is the thinking process that one discovers along the way. If you can understand the process for acquiring knowledge, you can then use that process to analyze and solve any potential problem. Renita and I used the thinking process that we learned in school long ago to help us advocate for Julia. It is a process that helped us when Julia was a baby and one that we still use today.

Some states use different terminology for the plans covered by IDEA. For example, in my state of Texas, an IEP is referred to as an ARD (Admissions, Review, and Dismissal) Plan. The principles are the same—to ensure that any child has access to services that will prepare him/her for future education, employment, and independent living. In short, the ability to be a productive citizen to the greatest extent possible. Many people are unfamiliar with these plans and think of them as some sort of "paperwork" that they must get through in order to enroll a child in school. On the contrary, these plans are the bedrock for the education of a child with special needs. One key thing to note is that the school doesn't get to just dictate what services they are willing to provide to a child. It is an opportunity for the parent and the school to work together to determine the services that are appropriate for the child. If, for example, a child is deaf and the school district doesn't have a deaf education program, the school must either create the program or send the child to a school that has such a program, at their expense. Once agreed to, the plan can be enforced the same as any other law. Because of our research, we recognized

Discerning God's Purpose

early on the importance of these plans and have always attended these meetings in person. Many times, we know more about the requirements under this law than the school officials who are governed by them. We are then able to use this knowledge to request the services that have greatly benefited Julia.

In addition to understanding the IDEA process, we also took the time to understand and select insurance plans that were most beneficial to Julia. Renita and I are generally in good health, and outside of the occasional doctor's visit or prescription, we really don't use our health benefits that much, however, we often select jobs that may pay less in salary but come with a generous benefit package that is beneficial for Julia. Over the years, our insurance plans have covered much more than doctor's visits. It has covered private therapy appointments, special summer camps (where therapy is involved), medical equipment, and even swim classes that were all designed to help Julia improve her body functionality so that she can survive as an independent adult. When Julia was a baby, we didn't know much about these plans, programs, and services so we started asking questions of those who do. We started by talking with the social worker at the hospital. Later, we talked to people in school districts who specialize in IDEA compliance, insurance agents, and service providers, researched data on the internet, attended conferences, and finally talked with lawmakers and their staffs at the state and federal level. When we started asking questions within a person's particular area of expertise, we found that people were more than willing to share their expertise. In an area that can be as obscure as IDEA and ADA guidelines, people are glad to see that someone is interested in their work. The good news is in talking with these people, we have also found out about other resources that are available free of charge or with minimal out-of-pocket expense. As the old saying goes, if you don't ask, you don't get.

With a little bit of effort, anyone can gain the knowledge necessary to better advocate for their child. We are not special. We just listened to God, took the time to gain a little wisdom, and stepped out on faith.

CHAPTER 8
UNDERSTANDING WHAT IS IMPORTANT

I remember when I was a young man in my twenties; I wasn't very focused in life. I was newly married, had just left active duty as an Army officer, and was trying to figure out what to do next. I had three jobs in less than six months. I remember going on an interview for an entry-level job at a prestigious company. I wasn't thrilled about taking it because I was still in the "I can conquer the world" stage that most people at that age go through. I remember sitting down and sharing my feelings with my Dad. His advice to me was very blunt. "Son, understand what's important. You are married now and have responsibilities. You have to have a job that will pay the bills. You will have time to do what you want later after you retire, but for now, it's time to grow up." While his advice was a cold slap in the face and I didn't agree with all that he said, the lesson that he was trying to impart was to recognize what was most important in my life and to work toward accomplishing that goal. I remembered his advice when Julia was born. She instantly became our number-one priority. She was going to require frequent medical appointments and had unique care requirements, so we decided to change our career goals and aspirations in order to take care of her.

After Renita was laid off, we decided that she would take a sabbatical for the first five years of Julia's life. Not wanting to abdicate my responsibilities as a dad, I rearranged my work schedule so that I could be home as much as possible in order to help out. The next year, after I was laid off, I decided to change careers so that I could remain a constant presence in her life. Soon afterwards, I decided to get my real estate license and start investing in real estate. I always had a dream of becoming a real estate investor. I read all kinds of books and looked at the latest infomercials about how I too could get rich by "fixing and flipping" a few properties. At the time, Donald Trump had just written his first book *The Art of the Deal*, and I dreamed of being just like him. Now was my chance. Soon after I got my license, I went to work trying to find, buy, fix, and rent homes. There was only one problem: I was not cut out to be a real estate investor. I hated heavy construction projects, plus the idea of having to chase down people who owed rent didn't appeal to me. Still, I had a family to feed so I tried to find projects that didn't require a large amount of construction and rented to tenants who qualified for Section 8 (a federal government housing program that pays the overwhelming majority of the rent on behalf of low-income tenants) whenever possible.

I stuck it out, and eventually started to grow the business. I hired contractors to handle the construction work and a property management firm to select tenants and collect the rents. I was able to concentrate on doing what I did best, locating potential properties, running the numbers and closing the deal. Things were starting to stabilize when a few months into the business, we hit a

CHAPTER 8

snag. Shortly before Julia turned two, we realized that there were not a lot of resources for deaf children in Cincinnati. Our local school district did all that they could, but the simple fact was that there were not a lot of kids in our area with Julia's unique set of challenges. There was a school for the deaf in Cincinnati, but it was private and the tuition was sky high (the cost was approximately $20,000 per year, and the school district was only willing to pay less than half of the bill). There was also the question of expectations. I recalled a conversation with one of the doctors during a visit to the NICU shortly before Julia was released from the hospital. She said that deaf kids "typically don't read above the fourth grade level and many have difficulty in school." She went on to say that while it was too soon to know the extent of Julia's developmental delays, Julia also would probably never be able to walk nor live independently for the rest of her life. She seemed to be telling us that we needed to set "realistic expectations" for Julia and that she would never be a high achiever. I was very respectful during the conversation, but in my mind I was thinking *to hell with that and to hell with you. I am going to do everything that I can to maximize Julia's potential.* I remember coming home and telling Renita what that doctor said. We agreed that if we couldn't help her one way, we would find another. Julia may not be perfect, but we would work and encourage her to be the best possible version of herself. At that moment, "find another way" became our family motto.

Since Julia would soon turn three, we wanted to look for other alternatives before she started school. We searched for other

ECE options by looking on the internet, talking to other parents, consulting with hearing and disability experts, attending conferences, and any other way that we could think of to find out what was available. While attending one conference, we came across a school in St. Louis, Missouri, that had a great track record of teaching deaf kids to talk. For the first time, we also heard about this thing called the cochlear implant (CI). According to FDA.gov, a CI is "an implanted electronic hearing device, designed to produce useful hearing sensations to a person with severe to profound nerve deafness by electrically stimulating nerves inside the inner ear." We wanted to learn more, but we also had strong reservations. Julia had a unique type of hearing loss called auditory neuropathy. In simple language, Julia could actually hear but not well enough to recognize speech. It's like trying to listen to a radio station that is slightly off frequency. Auditory neuropathy had been classified as a new type of hearing loss only a few years before, and there weren't many people who were familiar with it. With auditory neuropathy, hearing aids were of little use. It could amplify the sound, but it still wouldn't be clear enough to recognize speech. CIs had been used a few times on those with auditory neuropathy, but the data was still inconclusive. In our minds, doctors were still experimenting with CIs on people with this type of hearing loss and, like we said before, we didn't want Julia to be a guinea pig. Julia was making great strides in therapy and was trying to talk so we didn't want her to have an unnecessary setback. While we weren't ready to try a cochlear implant, the school thought that Julia had enough hearing where they could help her.

Discerning God's Purpose

CHAPTER 8

We needed to try something new, and this seemed about as good a place as any to start.

While the school was interested in working with Julia, there was only one catch. We needed to physically move to St. Louis since this was technically a pre-school program. While this was a private school and we would be there on a trial basis, the school agreed not to charge us tuition if we would help them recover funding through the local school district IFSP process. The only thing that we would need to pay for would be another preschool program located close by that would provide therapy services for her movement disorder (by now, she had formally been diagnosed with cerebral palsy). Since I still had post-employment COBRA (the Consolidated Omnibus Budget Reconciliation Act) insurance coverage, our out-of-pocket expenses would be reduced. Between both programs, Julia had a five-day-a-week commitment in St. Louis. The services that she would receive in St. Louis were far better than the ones that she had in Cincinnati, so we decided to make the move. Since I still had a business going in Cincinnati, we decided that I would make the six-hour commute on a weekly basis between Cincinnati and St. Louis. Since we didn't know how this would turn out, we decided to rent an apartment in St. Louis while continuing to maintain our home in Cincinnati. It was an expensive proposition to maintain two households, but Julia was our top priority. We decided to step out on faith and do what we could to help her.

Julia started the program and at first began to show some progress. She was starting to respond to additional sounds at school, and the therapy program showed promise as well. The school did everything that they could but without the cochlear implant, Julia's progress slowed. Within a few months, Julia hit a wall with her progress. Eventually, the school came to the conclusion that they could do nothing more for Julia, so after seven months, we found ourselves back in Cincinnati. In one way, this was good because the constant commute between the two cities was wearing me out. We knew that staying in Cincinnati wasn't an option given the lack of school resources that were available for Julia. Also, by now the economic recession of 2002 had started to set in and soon Cincinnati felt its effects. People were losing jobs, and those who didn't worried over an uncertain economy. As a result, the housing market also slowed down, which was not good news for my business. We moved to Cincinnati eight years before because of jobs, but now we found ourselves in transition. Although we adopted Cincinnati as our new hometown, we now had no jobs and no family support. Some of our friends had moved to other cities, and our church, which served as a critical foundation for us during our time of need, was now going through a change in leadership and was headed in a different direction. God seemed to be closing the door on our stay in Cincinnati. Still, we had a choice. We could stay in Cincinnati, try to find resources to help Julia, and at the same time fight to save a failing business or we could find somewhere else that was better suited for all of us. We knew what our purpose was so it was an easy decision. We decided to follow God's lead and prepared to leave Cincinnati. As painful as it was to close this chapter, we started the process of shutting down the

Discerning God's Purpose

CHAPTER 8

business and at the same time looked for a place to begin the next chapter in our lives.

We started searching for new schools and discovered Gallaudet University in my hometown of Washington, D.C. Gallaudet is a federally chartered private university that is primarily known as a school for the deaf and hard of hearing. I only knew a little about Gallaudet. It was a short distance from where I went to college and was frequently in the news (mostly for protests on campus). What I didn't know is that in addition to university programs, Gallaudet also operated ECE, elementary, and high school programs for deaf kids under the umbrella of the Clerc Center for Deaf education. The Clerc Center had available resources that were far and beyond anything that was available in Cincinnati. It contained a normal K-12 education program, as well as therapy services that were well suited for someone with Julia's needs. There was another benefit to Gallaudet as well. Most of our family was within a two-hour drive of the school. After both of us were laid off, both sets of parents were encouraging us to move closer to home so that they could help us care for Julia. They knew the heavy burden that we carried and wanted to help. Lastly, the Washington, D.C. area was the home for the federal government. I previously worked for Uncle Sam as a member of the military and also consulted with the government as a private contractor. I had many friends and family members who worked for the government, and there was a good chance that I could find employment. While the salary would be lower than in private industry, the government was a secure employer, had excellent benefits, and offered flexible hours so that I could continue to be an active and involved parent. We took a trip to D.C. and visited Gallaudet and the Clerc Center. The faculty evaluated Julia and found her to be an excellent candidate for the program and accepted her for enrollment beginning in the fall. Decision made. We were moving to Washington.

My parents graciously allowed us to live with them until we could find employment and a place of our own. The federal government is notoriously slow when it comes to hiring, so at first, I looked for any job that was available. Right after the move, I took a series of odd jobs in order to make ends meet until I could find something better. I worked such glamorous jobs as a night stock clerk at Target and a retail inventory specialist. My wife pitched in and took a job stocking greeting cards at a local supermarket. Quite a humbling experience for two people with advanced schooling, but we both recognized that Julia's wellbeing took priority. God never promised that our journey would be easy. We experienced some ups and downs; however, we were fulfilling our purpose and for us, that was most important.

Discerning God's Purpose

CHAPTER 9
HAVING COURAGE

As followers of Jesus Christ, sometimes God asks you to do things that are very difficult. Throughout the Bible, God shows that we can trust Him, that He has a plan and a purpose for each of us, and that He has us in the palm of His hand. He never said that life would be easy, yet He has always given us the power of choice. We can choose to follow His plan or our own. When I follow my own path, it seems that there are obstacles at every turn. Everything that can go wrong does go wrong and simple tasks are unnecessarily difficult. Yet, when I follow His path, it may not be easy, but it is effortless. In other words, there may be obstacles, but it feels like someone is right beside me helping to move them out of the way. It is as if things were meant to be. Things may sometimes seem dark but by praying and following His direction, we can have courage that things will always get better. We moved to Washington, D.C. with no jobs, no home, and only the courage that we were doing the right thing for our daughter.

I must admit, it was hard moving back home with my parents. Of course, we had visited many times, but I hadn't lived at home since returning from the Army. Renita and I moved into my old room while Julia slept across the hall in the guest room. I had become accustomed to being the man of the house, but now I was living under someone else's roof. My friends and family would never say anything in front of me, but I heard whispers about how, "I couldn't make it on my own and had to come home." It was a very humbling experience to say the least. I felt like King Solomon was talking about me when he wrote Proverbs 18:8 which says "The words of a whisperer are like delicious morsels; they go down into the inner parts of the body." There were many days when I wondered if I was doing the right thing. I didn't mind struggling but hated to do it in such a public way. During those dark times, I sometimes would walk into Julia's room while she was sleeping and just look at her. I would think back to those long nights in the hospital and remember when God told me what my purpose was. I also remembered that there are different seasons in life. Sometimes you are the blessing, and sometimes you are the one in need of a blessing. I was lucky enough to have parents who loved me and genuinely wanted to help. In the morning, I would get up and look in the mirror. I would remember my old Army ROTC instructor's words ("Suck it up, Buttercup."), then proceed to get dressed and start looking for work.

Shortly after Julia started school, I landed a job as a program manager with the federal government. A short while later, Renita was lucky enough to find employment with the government as well. With our employment situation now stabilized, we were able to look for a new church, as well as a home of our own. We found a house and settled in while continuing to work with the school to help Julia. Overall, things were going well. The only difficulty

Discerning God's Purpose

that we had with the school was communication. This was the first time that Julia attended a school that used American Sign Language (ASL) as its main mode of communication. Since we didn't know ASL, it was hard to directly communicate with some of Julia's teachers regarding her progress. We knew that we needed to learn ASL. Whenever we faced something new, we would say that it was "another opportunity for us to excel." Julia was learning ASL in her ECE classes, but for the rest of us, we went to ASL class every Saturday morning.

One of the benefits that Gallaudet offered was to teach students and their families ASL for free. Some parents didn't want to learn ASL for whatever reason, but as for us, we jumped at the chance. Not only did we sign up for class, but so did my parents. We all wanted to communicate better with Julia, so if her primary language was going to be ASL, then we all had to learn. While my in-laws didn't live in the D.C. area, they were still interested in learning ASL. They read basic sign language books and picked up a few simple signs so that they could communicate with their granddaughter. As for the rest of us, it was off to Saturday morning class. On our first day, we dropped Julia off at child care, and then headed off to our assigned room. When it was time to begin, the instructor walked into the classroom and we got right to work. The only problem from my perspective was that our instructor turned out to be a deaf person. When she started signing, I thought *how the heck am I going to do this?* I know that we were there to learn ASL, but didn't we need to start off in the kiddie pool before jumping in the ocean? Apparently not because our instructor got right down to business. On the first day, we learned the alphabet and how to count to ten. If there was any clarification needed, she wrote the information on the blackboard. No talking was allowed, only signing. We were immersed quickly in ASL. When we got home, oh did we have a good laugh when trying to practice our new language. It had been a long time since I had been in a classroom (even longer for my parents), and sometimes our fingers would get stuck in the wrong position. We unintentionally gave ourselves some universal signs but soon started to get the hang of it.

Renita turned out to be a better student than all of us, but we still managed to communicate effectively with Julia. Soon we were going to various events on campus, and we started being able to follow along in conversations with deaf people. In the class, not only did we get an education in ASL but also on deaf culture. In the hearing world, people tend to be very polite or low key. The deaf world is completely opposite. I'm not saying that deaf people are rude, but they are brutally honest. It is part of the deaf culture. Hearing people can use changes in voice or certain sounds to convey their true feelings, but deaf people can be explicit in describing their thought or feelings. One thing is for sure, they will definitely let you know what is on their mind. Let me give an example. A few years after moving to Maryland, we met a mom whose daughter attended the same school as Julia. They didn't live too far away, and soon, the two girls started getting together for playdates. One day, we hosted a playdate over at our house, and the mom asked us to drive her daughter home after they were finished. Well, Renita and

Discerning God's Purpose

CHAPTER 9

Julia took the girl home while I was out running an errand. When I returned home, Renita told me how she was so embarrassed when they took the girl home. When I asked what happened, Renita told me that upon entering the home, they saw that the house wasn't as tidy as the woman probably would have liked. While my wife was polite and didn't say anything, my sweet precious little daughter boldly told the woman that her floor was dirty and she needed to clean up. My wife almost passed out. After Renita started to apologize for what Julia said, the woman cut her off by saying, "No reason to apologize. I understand deaf culture too and she's right, the floor is dirty." While it may have been embarrassing, Renita got a real-life lesson in deaf culture. When communicating with someone who is deaf, don't be sensitive because they can be very blunt. On the other hand, you don't have to wonder what a deaf person is thinking, because they will come right out and say it. Sometimes, I think the hearing world can learn a thing or two from the deaf about transparency and honesty.

By taking classes from a deaf person, we were better able to understand deaf culture and thus were better advocates for Julia. We also understood some of the prejudices of the deaf community as well. Sometimes, we encountered deaf people who didn't want to interact with hearing people. They wanted to communicate with Julia but not with us. Our position was simple, if you wanted to deal with Julia, you had to deal with us. As a hearing person, initially it takes courage to deal with deaf people; however, Julia was still our child, we were her advocates and we were not going to let anyone push us around.

Over time, Julia became settled in at Gallaudet and started making progress. She learned how to sign and pretty soon began making friends. Other than her additional therapy requirements, she had a school schedule just like any other kid. She progressed through pre-school, kindergarten, and then "graduated" to the first grade. At her school, the pre-school and kindergarten program focused on the Reggio Emilia style of learning (where the child controlled some aspects of what he/she learned) while grades one to eight focused on a more traditional academic model. During the first grade, we noticed that Julia's teachers wanted to focus more on accommodating her deafness and less on her other needs. We knew that Julia was a bright girl, and we needed to accommodate all of her needs and not just focus on one thing. Since we had just moved a few years before, we were reluctant to move her again so we tried to work with the school to address our concerns. During the summer after Julia's first-grade year, we attended a deaf education conference in Texas that focused on educating the total person, not just the deaf person. While there, we met other parents who were in similar situations and were trying to find better education options for their children. During breaks, some parents told us of having to move their children every few years just to get the accommodations that they needed. We already knew what this was like having to move from Cincinnati to St. Louis and then to the Washington, D.C. area to find the services that Julia needed. Now, I was hearing that this roller coaster may very well continue. The good news is at the conference, we found out that there were many more options for deaf education in our area than we realized so if we felt the need to move Julia, we probably would be able to find a program that didn't require us to move as a family again. Still, we wanted to try to work things out at her current school if at all possible.

As Julia began the next school year, we notice that Julia had the same issues as the year before. She had the same teacher, the expectations hadn't changed, and Julia was starting to say that she was bored at school. When we mentioned something to the staff, one of the academic specialists pointedly reminded us that they were technically a demonstration school (meaning that the school is associated with the university and is primarily used for training, research, experimentation, and professional development) and weren't held to the same standards as other schools for the deaf. We also looked at the curriculum for that year and noticed that it came from another deaf school that had since moved on to something else. We couldn't put it off any longer. We knew that it was time for a change. The previous summer, after returning from the deaf education conference, we figured that sooner or later we probably would have to move Julia to another school so we started to look at other programs in the area. The state of Maryland, where we lived, had a nationally recognized deaf education program and one of the campuses wasn't too far away. We toured the school, asked that Julia be evaluated as a candidate for admission, and upon her acceptance, enrolled her at the beginning of the next quarter. Moving her in the middle of the school year wasn't ideal, but we felt that we couldn't wait any longer and risk having her fall further behind. It took a great deal of courage on our part but moving her to the new school was an important step in preparing Julia for her purpose in life.

Julia's new school got to work right away trying to catch her up. At school, she had a team of dedicated teachers, counselors, and therapists that we felt had Julia's best interest at heart. In addition, her new school was closer to a world-renowned hospital and rehabilitation center so we moved Julia's therapy sessions there to take advantage of the latest research studies as well. In time, we were able to revisit the CI issue as well. Research into auditory neuropathy had increased, and several hospitals were now implanting CIs in kids with this particular hearing loss. One hospital, Johns Hopkins, was known for its head and neck surgical research so we made an appointment for a consult. Johns Hopkins is a world-renowned teaching hospital that is associated with the Johns Hopkins University School of Medicine. One of the noted areas of the hospital is the Listening Center, which specializes in cochlear implants and rehabilitation. We saw their leading surgeon, Dr. John Niparko, who determined that Julia would be an excellent candidate for the implant. By this time, Julia was a little older and since this decision would affect her for the rest of her life, we decided to include her in the process of making the decision on whether to proceed.

Being implanted was a very big decision for Julia that took a great deal of courage for a number of reasons. One reason was cultural. There is a constant debate within the deaf community about the use of hearing technology. Some feel that deaf people should exclusively use sign language as their mode of communication

Discerning God's Purpose

while others are open to using technology to aid in communication. We understood that Julia was deaf and would have cultural experiences that Renita and I, as hearing people, would not and could never understand. However, for Julia, we have always emphasized her having the ability to understand, communicate, and function in both the deaf and hearing worlds. If she was to be prepared for whatever God had in store for her, she needed to be able to communicate in any setting. The second reason for courage was more medical. Because of her form of hearing loss, Julia technically wasn't completely deaf, but hard of hearing. She could hear some sounds but not enough to recognize speech. If she decided to go ahead with the surgery, she would lose all of her natural hearing ability. She would have to totally rely on the CI in order to hear anything. It was a case of taking one step back in order to take three steps forward. It was a tough decision, one that she thought about for weeks. In the end, she voted to receive CIs to be able to hear using both ears. It was a very courageous decision for someone who was entering those awkward pre-teen years, but Julia has always been a fighter and we raised her to think and make decisions for herself. Since Julia had to live with this decision for the rest of her life, we thought that it was only fair for her to make it. It wasn't easy, but in making this decision, Julia showed that she was well on her way to becoming the independent woman that we hoped she would be.

CHAPTER 10
DON'T SETTLE

When faced with opposition, many people choose to take the easy route and settle for something that is less than what they want. I remember that we once had to deal with a situation that quite frankly, pissed me off. When Julia was still in the NICU, we learned that she would probably experience developmental delays because of complications from her premature birth. When she was a toddler, she was formally diagnosed with a mild form of cerebral palsy (CP). There are a lot of misconceptions about what a CP diagnosis actually means. According to the Mayo Clinic, CP is "a disorder of movement, muscle tone or posture that is caused by damage that occurs to the immature, developing brain, most often before birth." There are different levels of CP with some people having virtually no outward signs of effects while others have severe impairments. Nonetheless, CP affects movement, not intelligence. As part of a normal school admissions process, students are often evaluated on their intelligence to see what class level he/she should be placed in. Julia was no different. When we transferred her to the new school in Maryland, Julia took an intelligence test and was found to have an average level of intelligence. What this meant was that while CP would affect her physical movements,

CHAPTER 10

she still had the capability to learn just like any other kid. From an educational point of view, the test revealed that there was no reason why she couldn't live a normal and productive life. She was and is capable of going to college if she wants and, through the use of adaptive technology, pursuing just about any career that she chooses.

Knowing this, we made a decision early on not to emphasize Julia's limitations but her abilities instead. We never used the words cerebral palsy or CP in talking about her challenges. We just told her that she had some unique challenges but that she could still do just about anything that any other child could do. The key, however, was that sometimes she would need to do things in a different way. We emphasized independence to Julia, and as a result, she was always a confident little girl. Growing up, she participated in dance, swimming, and other non-contact sports activities. She even participated in the Girl Scouts. The lesson we wanted to impress upon her was that she could accomplish anything she wanted as long as she had the determination to do it. Since moving her to the school in Maryland, Julia was getting good grades, and we were extremely happy with her progress. Then one day during the fourth grade, she came home and asked what the words cerebral palsy meant. When we asked why, she said that one of the therapists at school (I'll call her Jane) told her that she had CP. Renita and I looked at each other, but we still took the time to explain what it was. We also said that as far as we were concerned, her diagnosis didn't change anything. We still expected her to do her best.

Not too long after our conversation, we started noticing that Julia began asking for help more frequently. Before talking to Jane, she always insisted on doing things herself. Now, she wouldn't even try and just asked for help. When I would ask why, she said that Jane told her that because she had CP, she always needed to ask for help. She said that Jane said that there were things that she couldn't do and that she needed an aide in school who would be close by and available to help. All of a sudden, she wouldn't go to the bathroom by herself, wouldn't feed herself, wouldn't get dressed; in short she wouldn't do anything for herself. We always taught her to try to do things on her own first and if she couldn't, then ask for help. Now, she wouldn't even try. She just sat down and asked for help. That is when my blood started to boil.

Julia had always been fiercely independent. She knew that she needed some help; however, she never wanted to be singled out as being different from her classmates. When the teachers offered her a special chair for the classroom, she refused and used the same chair and desk combinations as the other kids. She did use a special mat on her desk and a keypad for tests, but other than that, she didn't want any other accommodations. When it was time to eat, she chose to eat foods where she could feed herself. She would use the same special mat that she had in her classroom to hold her plate in place and she would use a straw for her drink but that was it. She was adamant about not being fed in front of her classmates. When it came to the bathroom, she would ask the teacher's aide to take her to the family bathroom and would do everything that she could on her own and only ask for help when

CHAPTER 10

it was absolutely necessary. After her conversation with Jane, everything changed. She asked to have a single aide dedicated only to her. Whenever anything was difficult, she would just say "I can't do that. I have CP." She insisted that others do everything for her including bathing, dressing, feeding, and going to the bathroom. Her attitude changed at home as well. She was no longer interested in participating in physical activities. Instead of going out, she only wanted to stay at home and read or play on her iPad. It was as if she had given up and had accepted the label of cerebral palsy and all of the negative connotations that came with it. She was using CP as her crutch.

We were livid. After finding out what the therapist said, we went up to the school to meet with Jane, her supervisor, and the assistant principal. I'm afraid that I was not in the most professional of moods. My first inclination was to invite Jane to become a platinum member of the KMA club (Kiss My Assets), but since Julia still had to work with this woman, I refrained. I told them about the changes that we noticed, what Julia said, and asked how they could do something to take away the light in this kid.

Jane responded by saying that by law, Julia had a right to know about her diagnosis and the different services at her disposal. She and her supervisor also said that teachers were spending an inordinate amount of time accommodating Julia, and it was taking time away from the other kids. In addition, the teachers were complaining that Julia couldn't keep up with her schoolwork and recommended that her workload be reduced as an accommodation. They agreed that she needed additional accommodations and it was their duty to help her and to be "honest" with her about her limitations. I didn't know it at the time, but the school was setting us up for placing Julia on a "special needs track." By seeming to give up hope, Julia was playing right into their hands. She wanted to settle for being labeled a special needs kid.

All primary and secondary deaf education programs fall under the purview of special education for funding purposes; however, the deaf community doesn't look at being deaf as having a disability. They are proud of their culture and are quick to let you know that they are proud to be deaf. On the flip side of the coin are those who have additional challenges besides being deaf. In our experiences, those with additional challenges can be treated rather harshly. As with society in general, many deaf educators simply don't want to deal with anyone who has additional needs. No matter the circumstance, those with additional challenges tend to be placed in a special needs category where schools can get additional funding for educating the child while at the same time lowering the standards of instruction. In Julia's case, she wasn't being treated as an individual but like anyone else who needed an additional accommodation. Our feeling was that the school was making a case for getting more money and doing less work. Many kids in the special needs category don't graduate from high school but receive a certificate of attendance after they reach the age of twenty-two and are kicked out of the educational system. While this is an acceptable outcome for some, it wasn't for us. We weren't willing to settle for anything less than Julia doing her best. After the meeting, we came home and told her that we

Discerning God's Purpose

approved the use of a personal aide, but that she still needed to try her best. Our advice seemed to go in one ear and out the other. No matter how hard we tried, over the next year, her attitude stayed the same. When it was time for her to attend middle school, it was no surprise that the school recommended that she remain at the same campus.

Many deaf schools have dorms for kids who live too far away to commute to school on a daily basis. Since no one wants to have an elementary- or middle-school age child be away from home up to five days a week, some states divide their schools for the deaf into two campuses in order to keep as many of the younger kids as close to home as possible. When it is time for high school, many kids have a choice of staying at home and attending their local school district or staying in the dorm and attending the school for the deaf. Our state had a two-campus arrangement. There was an east and west campus and because of where we lived, Julia attended the east campus. The issue that we had is that each campus had its own curriculum and accommodation standards, which led to one campus (the west) being academically stronger than the other. While Julia would be required to attend the west campus for high school, the school recommended that she stay at the east campus in order to receive the services that she needed. Also, we were told that because of where we lived, their rules required Julia to stay at her current campus as long as possible. It seemed as if we were stuck. We wanted Julia to stay at home anyway so we approved the school's recommendation for her to attend middle school at the east campus.

It soon became evident that this decision was a mistake. Julia went from a grading system of As, Bs, and Cs, to a progress report based solely on the goals of her IEP. We knew of other kids from her elementary class who lived closer to the boundary for the other campus and were allowed to attend the west campus for middle school. The parents (and some teachers) that we talked to said that the difference in education at the other campus was night and day compared to what Julia received. She was on the special needs track and therefore wasn't subject to the academic rigors as kids attending middle school on the other campus. This track was focused on skills that helped her with the basic necessities of life but did little for her academically. It turns out that Renita and I were not the only ones who were unhappy with this decision. It soon became evident that Julia was becoming bored at school. Her teachers did little to challenge Julia to reach for the stars, and soon she became frustrated and started to act out. We started getting reports from the middle school principal and her therapist that Julia was starting to become a problem. She didn't want to cooperate during her therapy sessions and was crying during class. She was becoming disruptive and the school wanted our help to get Julia "back on the right track." They also wanted to send her to the school psychologist to see if she could recommend something to help Julia. I could see that they would soon be recommending medication to try to control Julia. In short, they wanted her to settle where she was and to learn to accept mediocrity. We had worked too hard to allow someone else to lower the goals for what Julia could achieve in life. It was time for another change.

Discerning God's Purpose

CHAPTER 10

By the spring of her first year in middle school, we had had enough. Through our channels in the deaf community, we were told that the east campus was indeed known as the "Special Ed" campus and that kids typically had a rough transition when it came time to attend high school on the west campus. Some kids were so far behind that they had to repeat the eighth grade on the west campus in order to get caught up. Renita and I decided to try to move Julia now in hopes that she could catch up academically and be ready on time for high school. We signed up to take a tour of the other campus and requested a meeting with the middle school principal. We took the tour and even saw some of the kids who had been in Julia's class the year before. The middle school principal thought that it would take some time but that he didn't see a problem with Julia being able to catch up. Next up was a meeting with the superintendent. When we requested a tour of the west campus, we also received an invitation to meet with the superintendent. He had already talked to the faculty from the east campus and was familiar with their recommendations for Julia. We explained that Julia had the intelligence to succeed in a regular academic environment and were interested in seeing if she could be placed at the west campus for the seventh grade. While the superintendent was respectful, he repeated the recommendations of the administrators at the east campus. He also reminded us that we lived in the eastern part of the state and said if we wanted to place Julia on the west campus, we needed to move into the boundary for that campus. Lastly, he explained that because of resource shortages, he didn't know if Julia's additional needs could be accommodated at the middle school on the west campus. They were trying to increase the number of therapy resources, but at that time, the best place to accommodate Julia right now was at the east campus.

We had a difficult decision to make for a number of reasons. First, we owned a home in an area of the state that was still recovering from the great recession that had hit many U.S. cities only a few years before. If we wanted to move Julia to the west campus, we were going to have to either rent out our current home or maintain two households, a very expensive proposition in the state of Maryland. I was getting nightmares thinking of our similar experience of only a few years before. Second, even if we did move her to the west campus, we would have fewer options in place to support Julia. While we were currently in a position to provide private therapy services to Julia, the distance to the west campus and the economic reality of maintaining two households would make this nearly impossible. Third was our employment. If we moved, our commuting time each way between work and home would double to almost two hours each way. Julia would have better academics, but we would have to arrange for before- and after-school activities or have her stay at home alone for a few hours (think latchkey kid) until we got home. Lastly, we would be further away from family and friends so we would essentially be on our own again.

On our way out, we noticed that the location of some of her classes would require Julia to walk to buildings that were up to a block away from the main campus. When we inquired about

Discerning God's Purpose

this, our tour guide told us that students typically walked to the other building in small groups and they hadn't had a problem. Since the west campus was more of an open campus (no security fence and the dorms and other buildings were accessible by anyone from the community), my security antenna went up. Julia did have additional challenges, so I was concerned that the other students would simply leave Julia behind and that she would be on her own and vulnerable in the community. After the tour and the meeting, Renita and I both had concerns about Julia attending the west campus. While we agreed that it was better academically, we had concerns about Julia's safety and our ability to provide the other services that she needed. In the end, we felt that we needed to find a better alternative for Julia. She was capable of succeeding on the regular academic track, and we wanted her to fulfill her true potential. It was time, once again, to move.

First we looked in the D.C. area, and then across the country, at different schools in terms of academic performance as well as their ability to accommodate Julia's needs. We kept coming across the Texas School for the Deaf that seemed to be perfectly suited for Julia. It checked our major requirements such as high educational standards, use of technology, inclusive student programs, and a secure campus. The only issue was that it was located in Austin, Texas, which was fifteen hundred miles away from where we currently lived. We were a little familiar with the school because we had attended the deaf education conference there about five years before. The school was consistently rated as one of the top deaf schools in the country and was known to be very innovative in terms of education. We also knew of the school superintendent because of her affiliation with Gallaudet University (she sat on the Board of Trustees), where Julia attended the ECE program years before. We decided to travel to Austin to take a tour of the campus and its middle school and, at the same time, get Julia evaluated as a candidate for admissions before the end of the current school year.

We took the trip to Austin and the Texas School for the Deaf, and it was all that we were hoping for and more. The middle school principal was very enthusiastic and showed us how they could accommodate Julia's needs while attending the regular academic program. The Student Services department showed us how they could accommodate Julia's therapy needs with minimal disruption to her core academics and showed us examples of how they accommodated students with similar challenges in the past. Next, the admissions office showed us their graduation rates and success rates of students who went on to college. Finally, the athletics department showed us how kids with additional challenges were able to participate in extra-curricular activities. Julia instantly became interested in cheerleading when she saw a picture of the current squad that included persons with special needs. At the end of the tour, we were convinced that this school was the right place for Julia. We headed home to figure out how we could relocate to Austin.

Our biggest hurdle, of course, was employment. We both had good-paying jobs and were reluctant to just walk away. Since

Discerning God's Purpose

CHAPTER 10

government officials are always talking about being family friendly, we wanted to see if there was a way that we could continue in our jobs while living in Texas. The government is not the most forward-thinking institution, so we knew that we would need to make a strong argument of how we could remain productive in Texas in order to make the move and keep our jobs. We both approached our employers from a position of strength. We had both been recently rated as outstanding employees and had excellent reputations within our respective offices. We gathered our job descriptions along with data on our work performance and went to see our respective supervisors. We explained our situation and proposed a solution that we thought would be a win/win for us and our respective organizations. We proposed to move to Texas and travel back to D.C. every other week at our own expense. We presented a plan of how we could complete our responsibilities, including how we would communicate with supervisors and coworkers and what types of reports we would give on a weekly basis. We also showed the cost to the organization in lost time and productivity if we were forced to leave (the government typically takes approximately one year to replace an employee who has left and then takes another six to nine months for the new person to become proficient in the job). We really didn't want to leave but nonetheless, we still needed to make the case of what would happen if we did.

In the end, both employers recognized our value and approved our plans to work alternatively between Washington, D.C.

and Texas. It would be a huge financial sacrifice but one that we were willing to make. We wanted to give Julia the best education option that we could and didn't want to settle for anything less. We prayed for guidance and finally made a decision. We were moving to Texas.

Discerning God's Purpose

LIVING IN MY PURPOSE

Former football coach Jimmy Johnson was famous for telling his players, "If you talk the talk, you gotta walk the walk." My Dad had an equally famous saying. "Talk is cheap," he would say. "Actions speak louder than words." In everyone's life, there comes a time when you have to stop thinking about something and actually get up the courage to do it. For me, this was by far the hardest part of my journey. In deciding to move to Texas, we made a decision to leave everything and everyone that we knew behind, leave our comfort zone, and go forward based solely on our faith in God. No, we weren't going to the other side of the earth, but we were leaving the bonds of family to commit to living in a new environment. It reminds me of the story of Elisha in the Bible. In 1 Kings, chapter 19, Elisha leaves his home and everything he knows and follows the Prophet Elijah. He didn't do this because Elijah promised Elisha fame, fortune, or world adoration. He did it simply because Elijah approached him in the field and told him to come. Elisha felt so strongly about following him that right in the middle of plowing a field, he burned his oxen, ran to tell his parents goodbye, and left with Elijah. This story is important to me because just like Elisha, I felt strongly that God was leading me to take action.

I was trusting God to protect me and my family, and like Elisha, depended on God to be faithful to His promise.

While I really didn't want to move, I knew that Julia couldn't continue to excel by remaining where she was. After looking at all of our options, we knew we really didn't have a choice. I remembered my assignment to prepare Julia for whatever God had planned for her. What I didn't know at the time was that later, God would use Julia to expand my purpose in ways that I could never imagine. This is not to say that my faith in God's plan was total. I must admit that I didn't totally trust Him. There were times where I was stubborn. When that happened, God would close doors and use stressful situations to get my attention. Eventually, I remembered an old tale that says "your arms are too short to box with God" and surrendered to His will. When I let go and let God mold me on His potter's wheel, I finally found a level of understanding that allowed me to embrace my purpose, which lead to a new calling.

CHAPTER 11
THE MOVE TO TEXAS

We didn't know anyone in Texas. We literally moved on a wing and a prayer. We felt certain that Julia's new school would provide the help that Julia needed, but we had been on this moving train before. Since we didn't know if this would be a short-term or a long-term solution, we decided to hedge our bets by keeping our home in the D.C. area while renting a home in Texas. Even though it made sense financially to immediately rent out our house in Maryland, we decided to hold off at least until the end of the year, just in case things didn't work out. Renita and I decided to alternate our trips back to Maryland so that one of us would always be in Texas with Julia. To reduce the effects of maintaining two households, we did everything that we could to hold down expenses.

My parents really helped us in our situation by graciously allowing us to stay with them whenever we returned to the area for work. By staying with them, we wouldn't need any of our household items, so we decided to take everything with us to Texas. By not keeping anything in the house, we could rent out our house pretty quickly if things worked out in Texas. Initially, the plan was to rent an apartment close to campus while putting the majority of our belongings in storage. That plan changed when we saw that over a hundred people a day were moving to Austin to take advantage of the technology boom that the city was experiencing. As a result, the cost to rent an apartment wasn't that much different from renting a house. Factor in the cost of storage, and it was actually cheaper for us to rent a house than to go into an apartment. We decided to go down to Austin in July for a house-hunting trip found a nice home to rent that wasn't too far from the school yet still a convenient commute to the airport (since we would be flying back to D.C. on a regular basis). We came back, packed up, said goodbye to our friends and family, and in late August made the three-day drive to Austin. I drove the moving truck while my wife drove one of our cars with Julia and our dog. Since we took all of our belongings to Texas, we took my parents up on their offer to stay with them when we were in town for work since our house was now empty. We were on our way.

The trip to Austin was interesting to say the least. I forgot to tell my bank that I was traveling cross country so while traveling in Arkansas, the bank froze my credit card account thinking that it had been stolen. I spent an hour on the phone at a gas station in the middle of nowhere trying to get the bank to unfreeze the account. When we hit Texas, we experienced heat like we had never seen. Texas was in the middle of a prolonged heatwave. They had over a hundred days of one-hundred-plus degree temperatures, and we were driving into that. While the air conditioning in the vehicles worked fine, the heat still came blazing through the windows so we had to take frequent breaks in the middle of the day just to get a break from the sun.

While on the road, I received an email from my boss saying that someone up the management chain was objecting to my new commuting arrangement. I was a little taken aback because I had followed proper protocol by informing my chain of command and receiving approval before committing to the move. Even the office of human resources, charged with enforcing agency policy and federal law regarding any change in work assignments or location, reviewed the proposed arrangement prior to final approval and had no objection.

Most surprising of all, the senior official objecting to the arrangement was five levels above me in the chain of command and had little direct contact with me. Since the agency encouraged telework (and other alternative work schedules) with no financial impact to the government (I would travel between Austin and D.C. at my own expense), I was very surprised that he was involved. Needless to say, with all of our possessions in the truck, our commitment to a one-year lease on the house in Texas, and Julia committed to starting a new school in a few days, returning to Maryland at this point was not an option. After we arrived and got settled, I called my boss and reminded him of our agreement. I also said that we had incurred a significant expense based on the agency's approval and that it was too late for us to reverse course now. To his credit, my boss said that he would talk with the senior official and try to work something out. For now, he said, everything would stay in place as previously agreed to. I hung up the

CHAPTER 11

phone and did the only thing that I could do—hope and pray for the best.

As it turns out, both of our employers began to have second thoughts over the new work arrangement. There was no question that both of us were exceeding expectations regarding our work responsibilities. In the coming months, both of us continued to receive excellent evaluations and were repeatedly complimented on the quality of our performance. Yet, some in management just had the mentality that we should be physically present on a daily basis. At first, we would hear comments from co-workers about someone not being satisfied with our arrangement. Next, we heard supervisors make remarks in management meetings about reviewing the arrangement to ensure that it was "still working for both parties." Finally, after about six months, things started to come to a head. It all started with Renita's employer. Her boss sent an email formally requiring her presence in the office on a full-time basis. There was no mention of missed assignments or dereliction of duty, just a demand to return to her previous schedule. I also knew because of comments that I heard from my boss that a similar demand would probably come to me in the not-so-distant future.

This requirement put us in quite a precarious position. We moved to Texas for Julia to attend the Texas School for the Deaf. She was working hard, making progress, and started to enjoy school again. She even made the honor roll for three straight quarters. We were starting to see some of her confidence return as she realized that she was capable of keeping up with her peers. Like most parents, we would occasionally have doubts about the course that we took regarding Julia's education and the impact that it had on our family. In our case, all doubts were erased when we all returned to Maryland for a family visit during her spring break. Julia wanted to see her friends at her old school so we stopped in for a visit. Since school was in session, we had short visits with her old friends in the classroom. We had an eye-opening experience in one class when the teacher was covering a topic that Julia had learned during her first few months of school in Texas. She knew the topic and was able to summarize the lesson for her classmates. The best part came after we returned home from our trip, Julia told us that she now understood why we moved her to a new school and thanked us for looking out for her. Now, with Julia doing so well at her new school, we weren't about to disrupt her progress. Since I was still required to return to D.C. every other week to fulfill my on-site work requirement, and if Renita was required to be in D.C. full-time, who would take care of Julia when I was gone? To top it all off, with everything going so well, we had just put down a sizeable deposit to purchase a home in Texas and had also just rented out our house in Maryland. Even if we wanted to come back, we couldn't (at least not without incurring significant expenses). It looked as if one of us might have to quit our job in order to fulfill our purpose. We weren't going to turn our lives upside down because of office politics. After reviewing our options, we discovered that her agency was actually violating the Americans with Disabilities Act of 1990 and the Rehabilitation Act of 1973 by making this demand. While we were not disabled,

Discerning God's Purpose

CHAPTER 11

we were the primary caregivers of a minor child who was, and therefore, we were also covered under both acts.

Renita replied to the email, reminded her boss of her exemplary performance and based on her status as the main caregiver for a disabled child, requested a further review. Luckily, an official further up in the management chain, looked at the facts and decided to try to find a solution that would work for both parties. In the end, Renita was able to remain with her employer; however, she transferred to another position that was better suited for working full-time in Austin. She was able to stay in her career field but allowed to expand her focus by taking on new and challenging assignments at a higher level. It was a win for both parties. While I was happy for her, the situation with my employer ended far differently.

While Renita and I both worked for the federal government, we worked for separate agencies, with a different set of rules, and managers who interpreted those rules very differently. After nine months of commuting back and forth under my new arrangement, I was still hearing rumors of how this senior official was still not satisfied with my telework arrangement. By now, I had a new boss, and he was told in no uncertain terms that my telework agreement should be cancelled. To his credit, my boss judged me on the merits of my work and responded that he had no issues with my agreement. My second-line manager even went so far as to ask my fellow managers if my schedule posed a problem (all said no). Finally, I had enough of the innuendo and back channel comments so I requested a meeting with this particular official to find out just what was going on. I gathered my performance data and set off for the meeting. No sooner had I sat down than this official told me that he was ordering me to return to work full-time in Washington, D.C. within the next two months. He told me that any time that I was away from the office required me to take leave. When I tried to state my case regarding the quality of my work and that there were no signs that my telework agreement had caused a problem, he cut me off. He said that he just didn't believe in managers working remotely and that he wanted everyone in the office and available so that if there was a problem, we could "get into a room and just figure it out." It didn't matter what I said, his mind was made up. If I wanted to keep my job, I needed to return to D.C. full time.

This was the moment of truth. God wanted to see if I would really trust Him, and I'm afraid that I failed the test. I was afraid that if I left my job, my family would be broke and out on the street. Instead of praying for guidance, I decided to "help God out" by trying to work things out for myself. Since Renita was now in Austin full time, we decided that I would live in D.C. during the week and return home to Austin on the weekends. It wasn't ideal, but we felt that it was the best option at the time. Soon, I found myself traveling between D.C. and Austin on a weekly basis with very few breaks. Since Julia still needed assistance, I was approved for leave under FMLA so that I could stay home for a few days every month and care for Julia. I also used the time to recover. Being on the road every week takes a toll on the body. No matter

Discerning God's Purpose

how good you are, everyone needs to take time out and rejuvenate yourself.

Since I wanted to do things my way, God stepped back and said go ahead. It was very evident that I couldn't keep this pace up for a long period of time. I started getting sick, was tired all the time, and traveled so much that at one point, I began to question whether I lived in Maryland or in Austin. I had failed the test. One thing about God, though, He always gives you a chance to make it up. He keeps bringing you to the same challenges until you finally pass the test.

CHAPTER 12
RESTORATION

Julia is a surviving triplet, having lost her only brother and sister within a span of ten days. During the early part of her life, Renita and I were consumed with Julia's health and wellbeing. Between doctor and therapy appointments, multiple moves, and doing all that we could to ensure that she got a great start in life, we never had a chance to talk to Julia about what happened to RJ and Jamie. She noticed three pictures at home and at her grandparents' houses that looked very similar to her when she was a baby, but as often happens, the catalyst for the conversation came from school. It started when she attended the demonstration school on Gallaudet's campus. Julia started noticing that her classmates had brothers and sisters and wondered why didn't she? Her curiosity only intensified after she moved to the elementary school in Maryland. She would see their siblings when a parent would come to pick up a classmate or when she was invited to birthday parties, playdates, and the like. One day, when she was either in second or third grade and still attending elementary school in Maryland, Julia came home and asked us why she didn't have a brother or a sister. Renita and I looked at each other and thought that the time had come to tell her what happened. I think that she was seven

CHAPTER 12

or eight at the time, and we knew that this was going to be a hard conversation; however, she had a right to know.

Since we didn't want this to be a rushed conversation, we set aside some time on a Saturday to tell her what happened. Just like anyone else, Julia grieved for her siblings even though she had only known them for a short time. Over the next year or so, we would occasionally see her tear up when thinking about RJ and Jamie. We supported her by saying that it was fine for her to express her feelings of sadness but that it was important to remember that RJ and Jamie would always be in her heart. We talked of them often and reminded her that she could always talk to them through prayer. Not too long after, I remember waking her up one morning to get her ready for school only to find her giggling and laughing as if having a grand old time. The ironic thing is that Julia is not a morning person. It was and is usually very hard to get her up in the morning, but this morning was totally different. She woke up with a smile on her face like none I had ever seen. When I asked why she was so happy, she said that she dreamed that she was playing with RJ and Jamie! That morning, you could have knocked me over with a feather.

Julia seemed to be coming to terms about her brother and sister being in heaven. Renita and I didn't understand why RJ and Jamie were with us only for a short while, but we always said that God knows best. Renita and I were only children so we just thought that it was our lot in life to raise an only child. We were a little older now and knowing that we didn't want to go through the whole pregnancy thing again, thought that our period for having additional children had passed. While we may have given up, Julia had other plans. When she was about nine or so, she started saying that she wanted a brother and sister and asked us if we could "find" some for her. We kept saying that we loved her, and that she was very special to us, but that maybe God had other plans. Besides, we would say, you still have your brother and sister up in heaven. Julia was not to be deterred. By now, she was in the fifth grade and was still asking us to find her a brother and sister. Not wanting to deal with the issue any more, Renita and I started telling her to pray about it. Soon, we were seeing Julia on her knees praying for God to send her a brother and a sister. We thought that it was cute, but being the great people of faith that we are (ahem), thought that there was as much chance of her having a brother and sister as there is of finding a man in the moon. We figured that we had a great life, had finally settled in our careers, and with all of the difficulties that we experienced in raising Julia with her unique challenges, we really weren't interested in having additional children.

We firmly believe that Julia is still with us today because of her fighting spirit. She fought to survive in the NICU and has been a fighter ever since. Although she did experience times when she felt helpless and trapped in her body, she would still fight for what she believed in. Whenever we would say no, that made her try that much harder. The same was true for her quest to have a brother and sister. She was respectful but very persistent. When we told her to pray about her request, she became a persistent petitioner of the Almighty. Once she decided to throw God in the conversation,

Discerning God's Purpose

CHAPTER 12

I should have known that the playing field would change. Julia had just finished elementary school and, despite our misgivings, was about to start her first year at the middle school in Maryland. One evening, Renita came home and after finishing dinner and putting Julia to bed, she told me that she had been thinking about adoption as a way to expand the family. What?! Where did this come from? She said that Julia got her thinking about children, and she was interested in adopting a child. She wanted a boy or a girl who was older than an infant (we were a little too old to go through the baby stage again) but would still be younger than Julia (she wanted to maintain Julia's status in the birth order). Besides, she said, we had been blessed with financial stability and maybe we could do our part and help a child in need. We always saw stories on the news of children waiting for adoption, so maybe we could help a child in need and bless Julia with the sibling that she wanted all at the same time.

Oh boy, I thought. Here we go. Just when I thought my life was settled, here Renita goes trying to upset the apple cart. I still wasn't interested, but, as the saying goes, happy wife, happy life. I told her to start checking into the process and to let me know what she found. What harm could it do to find out a little more about the adoption process? Little did I know the changes were about to occur.

I must admit that like all fathers, I always longed to have a son. I love my daughter dearly, but I was always a little jealous when I saw a father playing catch with his son or cheering on his kid in little league. Although I still wasn't convinced that we were meant to have additional children, I was beginning to get intrigued by the idea. Still, God had blessed us with Julia, and we had our hands full just dealing with her. Nevertheless, I remained open to Renita looking into the process. We started by looking at a D.C. area news station, which featured a weekly segment called "Wednesday's Child." They would showcase a child from the local area who was in foster care and available for adoption. After the segment, the reporter would provide a telephone number and a website for additional information. One day, Renita saw a teenage girl who really seemed to be looking for a "forever" family. Renita called the number and was told about an upcoming information session on the adoption process. Renita told me about it, and I agreed to attend.

We decided to ask my parents to take care of Julia while we went to the meeting. We weren't too keen on telling anybody where we were going (nor did we want to get Julia's hopes up) so we just said that we had a business meeting to attend. When we arrived, we picked up some of the handouts that they had, found a seat, and waited for everything to get started. The meeting was sponsored by the county Department of Social Services, and it was clear from the beginning that they were looking for people to serve mainly as foster parents. The representatives kept talking about the amount of money that a family could earn by agreeing to be a foster parent, what the requirements were and so forth. Foster care is for those children that the county eventually hopes to reunite with their birth family. While that is an admirable goal for some, I wasn't interested in having a revolving door for children

Discerning God's Purpose

to come in and out of our home. When I asked about the process for adoption, one of the representatives described an arduous process that a family would need to go through before being considered for adoption. Primarily, we were told that in Maryland, a family must agree to serve as a foster family first and then, if there is no hope for the child to return to the birth family, the family could petition the court for adoption. She continued to talk about the process for foster/adoption, but as far as I was concerned, the meeting was over. I knew that if I brought someone in our home and started the process of incorporating the child into our family life, only to see them pulled out and returned to their birth family, it would do us more harm than good. I had no interest in being on an emotional roller coaster with a child and only being considered for adoption as a last resort. If that was the plan then no thanks. Renita shared my feelings, so it was back to square one.

Around the time that Julia started middle school, we heard about an upcoming adoption fair being held at our church. When we first moved to Maryland, as is our custom, we made it a priority to find a church home. We looked for a church that was large enough to accommodate all of our needs but small enough where we wouldn't be overwhelmed and would easily get lost. With so many choices in our immediate vicinity, we tried a few different churches in search of just the right fit.

Early on, we were welcomed into the Judah Temple A.M.E. Zion church family. It was a small congregation that made us feel right at home. While there, we were overjoyed when Julia made the decision to give her life to Christ. One of the highlights of our stay was watching Pastor Moore baptize our daughter and start her on her journey of faith. While we loved Judah Temple, we needed to find a church that could better accommodate our family's needs. Julia was interested in learning more about Christ so we needed to find a church with a thriving deaf ministry. We finally found something that suited us at the First Baptist Church of Glenarden. Pastor John Jenkins was (and still is) a dynamic preacher who built a large congregation and a national reputation based on his goal of developing dynamic disciples yet created an environment that ministered to the needs of individual members. One area that members expressed interest in was adoption so the church held an adoption fair every year and invited state agencies and private adoption services to come and talk about the various methods of adoption.

On this particular day, I was tied up with another function, but Renita decided to go and check it out. Truth be told, I wasn't all that excited about going anyway. I remembered that last information session and didn't think that this one would be any different. Since I had another obligation, I was more than happy to skip this particular event. When Renita came home from attending the fair, she said that indeed the same representatives from the county were there trying to drum up support for foster care; however, she also said that there were other people there who were talking about international and private adoptions. Initially, I wasn't enthused. I knew of people going to Russia or China to adopt kids out of orphanages and heard about the rough conditions that these kids grew up in. Some of the people spent years

Discerning God's Purpose

CHAPTER 12

trying to undo the damage that these kids suffered while growing up in such conditions. On top of that, the whole reason that I even agreed to consider adoption was because there were kids out there who looked like me and desperately needed help. I had also heard that international adoptions were very expensive, and I wasn't sure that going that route was a viable alternative.

When I voiced my objection, Renita said that it wasn't like that at all. She told me of a meeting that she had with a wonderful person (I'll call her Penny) from a private adoption agency located right in our home state. Her agency focused on kids from Caribbean island nations with governments who were friendly to U.S. adoptions. She explained the general process of international adoptions and how it differed from the process of our home state. This was starting to look promising. These kids would not be "at risk" adoptions but were permanent placements. We decided to make an appointment to continue the conversation with Penny and learn more about the process and the children who were currently available.

By now, Julia was in the sixth grade, and we started to experience the difficulties with the middle school in Maryland. We thought that we would move Julia to the west campus and therefore be staying in Maryland so we decided to continue the adoption conversation with Penny. After we made the decision to move to Texas, we were disappointed because our discussions with Penny were starting to prove fruitful. We thought that we would once again have to start over after getting settled in Texas. When we told Penny what was going on, we were delighted to learn that we would be able to continue to work with her since her agency was able to provide adoption services in Texas. They would partner with other agencies for home inspections, background checks, and the like; however, Penny would remain our main point of contact just as if we were still there. Ultimately, we put the adoption discussion on hold until we could get settled in Texas and had a sense of our future.

After moving to Texas and with Renita's employment situation now settled, we contacted Penny and told her that we were ready to move forward with the adoption process. About a month after expressing renewed interest, Penny called to tell us about a little boy who might soon be available for adoption in a country called St. Vincent and the Grenadines (St. Vincent). We had never heard of the country, but Penny told us that she was very familiar with the country and their standards for adoption. She told us a little more about the boy, his background, and why he might be available for adoption (he recently lost his mother).The local adoption agency was still assessing his family situation and his suitability for adoption so Penny told us for now just to relax and wait until she had more information. The suitability assessment is critical because it involves a basic physical and mental exam to see if a child would meet the basic eligibility requirements for adoption. It also ensures that a child doesn't have any physical ailments or emotional baggage that would put a new family at risk. Most countries do this as a matter of routine since reputable outside adoption agencies will insist on seeing the results before engaging prospective parents. In the case of this little boy, the local adoption

Discerning God's Purpose

board determined that the boy would not be a good candidate for international adoption but would be better served by staying with his existing family. While we were disappointed by the determination, we fully understood the board's decision. Since another child could become available at any time, we decided to do what we could and get a jump on the initial adoption paperwork (the part that would just involve information on our family) so that we would be ready when the next call came.

A few weeks later, Penny called us about another boy *and* a girl who might be available from the same country. It seems that these two siblings had just entered into foster care and were undergoing a suitability determination for adoption, but that so far, it looked like they would be made available. When we started this process, we told Penny that we were looking for a child (boy or girl) who was between five and ten years old. We wanted someone who was younger than Julia (we wanted to maintain the proper birth order with Julia still being the oldest), but didn't want a huge gap in age. From what Penny was telling us, these children met the requirements that we were looking for. Their names were Lezroy and Neilah and were nine and eight years old, respectively. While they could be adopted individually, the country's adoption board was making every effort to place them together since they were siblings. It seemed that God was hard at work answering Julia's prayer.

While this was the answer to Julia's prayer, I wasn't sure that it was the answer to mine. My purpose was to prepare Julia for whatever plan God had in store for her, and I didn't see how this was going to help. Julia had just turned thirteen, but because of her challenges, she was still a handful by herself. I didn't know how all of this was going to work out. I shared my concerns with Renita, and she responded by saying that if this is God's will, everything would work itself out. She told me to have an open mind and receive whatever blessing God had in store for us. Wise words from a virtuous woman.

A few days later, we were at church and our pastor confirmed what Renita was saying by speaking about how God always restores whatever is stolen from us. He shared the story of Job and how God allowed Satan to test Job by taking away his fortune (Job 1:13-17), his family (Job 1: 18-19), and even his health (Job 2: 7-9). While Job felt sorry for himself, endured the condemnation of his friends, and even argued with God, he didn't sin. This was a test that he passed with flying colors. In the end, God restores all that is taken from Job plus gives him a double portion of what he had before (Job 42: 7-17). During the sermon, I remember thinking about RJ and Jamie. When they died and went to heaven, I remember thinking that our assignment was to raise this only child. God had other plans. For years I carried a shame of having lost two children, and Renita always felt she did something "wrong" and God used the pregnancy to somehow punish us. The Bible, however, says something different. Isaiah 61:7-9 says:

> "Instead of your shame there shall be a double portion; instead of dishonor they shall rejoice in their lot; therefore in their land they shall possess a double portion; they shall have

Discerning God's Purpose

everlasting joy. For I the LORD love justice; I hate robbery and wrong; I will faithfully give them their recompense, and I will make an everlasting covenant with them. Their offspring shall be known among the nations, and their descendants in the midst of the peoples; all who see them shall acknowledge them, that they are an offspring the LORD has blessed."

In seeing these verses, I realized that God always restores. I knew that these two children were meant to be ours. I took Renita's advice and just started praying for God to direct my steps. Soon afterwards, we received word that both children were certified as being eligible for adoption. We let Penny know that we were indeed interested in adopting both children. Our two new children were on their way.

CHAPTER 13
ST. VINCENT

Once we indicated interest, the next step was arranging a visit so that we could meet the children. St. Vincent is a small Caribbean island nation that consists of a chain of islands that lie between Saint Lucia and Barbados. The children were located on the main island, just outside the capitol city of Kingstown. To get there, we would have to fly to either Barbados or Trinidad and then take a small commuter plane (Renita called it a puddle jumper) onto the island. Before going, we were warned that St. Vincent was one of the most impoverished nations in the Caribbean and wasn't like other islands where we had previously vacationed. It is best described as a remote country with little tourism activity and an educational system that is not very advanced. The official language of the country is English, however most people spoke something called Vincentian Creole, sort of a mix between English and the local island dialect so it is very hard for outsiders to understand. The island has no extensive opportunities for higher learning so some are required to travel abroad for an education. The adoption board does a good job in finding stable families to serve as foster parents so Lezroy and Neilah were located in a nice home in a rural community in the hills above Kingstown. They were made

CHAPTER 13

available because their mother decided to voluntarily place them into foster care. She was having a very difficult time providing a stable home and simply wanted a better life for them. By the time we visited them, their mother had formally renounced her parental rights and with no other family members claiming parental responsibility, the children were cleared for adoption.

After receiving a preliminary determination of suitability as adoptive parents, we traveled to St. Vincent to meet them and decide if we wanted to proceed with the adoption. We traveled in late September, which was after the beginning of school for Julia; however, we felt strongly that Julia needed to be involved in the process and have an opportunity to express her opinion before we made a final decision. We let Julia's school know what was going on and arranged for her to make up any missed assignments upon our return. Since we didn't know the living conditions that we would be faced with on the trip, we didn't take any of Julia's schoolwork with us. We made our flight arrangements, made sure that our passports were ready to go, and prepared to meet our new children.

Because St. Vincent is such a small island, all of our travel options showed that it would take two days to get there from Austin with a layover in either Toronto or Miami. Since we would be traveling to the east coast anyway, instead of staying in Toronto or Miami, we decided to fly to Maryland and see my parents for one night and then get up the next day and fly out of D.C for our travel to St. Vincent. We left Austin on a Monday and arrived in St. Vincent on Tuesday around eight at night. After leaving D.C, the fastest route had us going through Toronto to Barbados where we switched to a commuter flight for a short twenty-minute flight into St. Vincent.

I'll never forget that flight into St. Vincent. At the time, there was only one airline that serviced St. Vincent, as well as several smaller islands in the area, so it uses an island hopper flight schedule for these islands (that's a nice way of saying that the airline flies when it wants to, where it wants to, and isn't necessarily bound by the schedule). Since St. Vincent is a remote island, residents occasionally have to travel by air to visit friends and relatives on nearby islands and to pick up supplies that are not available locally. Consequently, this flight was packed with people and supplies (including a variety of fresh food). We were lucky that this flight was reasonably close to being on time. We boarded, received an abbreviated version of a safety briefing, heard the rumble of the propellers coming to life, and soon were headed toward the runway. Everything was fine until right before take-off, the flight attendant came through the cabin spraying something. (It wasn't air freshener but something different. I still don't know what it was.) The plane had two seats on each side of the isle. After the flight attendant was finished, Renita and I looked at each other and said a prayer for deliverance. Soon we took off and because the plane was so small, we felt every bit of turbulence. There was no inflight beverage service so I was glad that St. Vincent was the first stop. On our approach, the wind started to pick up, so we started rocking and rolling all over the place. After another prayer for our wellbeing, we landed without much difficulty. We got off the plane, grabbed our bags, went through immigration, and then

Discerning God's Purpose

CHAPTER 13

eased outside to find our driver. The adoption agency that we worked with was very experienced with adoptions on this particular island, so they helped us by arranging for a dedicated driver for the entire length of our stay. We later learned that the amount that we paid for our service (very reasonable by U.S. standards) was more money than most residents receive in a month. The driver picked us up from the airport and carried us to the hotel which was about twenty minutes away.

Although we made reservations and paid for our hotel well in advance, we found out that the bartering system is alive and well in St. Vincent. When we got to the front desk, we were first told that we didn't have a reservation. When we produced the reservation number, the front desk clerk confirmed the reservation but then quoted us a rate that was quite a bit higher than what we had reserved. Since I already paid for the room in advance, I had no interest in paying the higher rate. The clerk then said that since we made the reservation using American dollars, we were required to pay a conversion rate. On and on she went with additional fees. I was tired after the long trip and by now more than a little angry so I asked to see the manager. Out came a lady whom I later learned was the owner of the hotel. After I explained who I was, why I was on the island (along with the person who recommended their hotel) and what was happening, she confirmed the rate that I previously agreed to and agreed to "waive" the normal conversion fee. She then proceeded to tell us about the amenities located on property that were at our disposal, for a small fee of course. With that, she called to a person behind us who showed us to our room.

Because of the cultural environment and heavy European influence of the island, the hotel room was very sparse and had few amenities. It looked like something from the 1960s. Although we traveled to St. Vincent in early fall, the island was located in the southern Caribbean; therefore, the weather was still hot. Most American hotels would have the air conditioning running full blast so that the guest would be comfortable upon arrival. Not so at this hotel. When we entered the room, it felt like we had entered a sauna. We were hot, tired, and cranky after our experience with the front desk and now we had to deal with this. We looked around the room and found the air conditioning unit. Like everything else in the room, it was small and old. We cranked it up to full blast, but the room was still very slow to cool down. We were also hungry. We hadn't had anything to eat or drink since a late lunch in Barbados and didn't think to grab something for later. Our driver had left for the evening, and the hotel was quite a walk from the closest town. Being unfamiliar with the island, I was not about to entertain the thought of walking to town at night in order to grab something to eat. We called down to the front desk, and the clerk said that their restaurant was still open so we ordered room service for dinner.

This dinner was definitely an interesting experience. The menu contained dishes that I had never heard of, so in order to be safe, I ordered a ham and cheese sandwich with a bottle of water for each of us. After we finished our meal, we settled in and tried

Discerning God's Purpose

CHAPTER 13

to get some rest. We were to spend the next two days with Lezroy and Neilah at the home of their foster parents (for privacy sake, I'll refer to them as the Otters), so we needed our rest. We went to bed and tried to go to sleep, but it was simply too hot. I got up every so often to see if the air conditioning unit was still working. After a few hours, the room started to cool down and we were finally able to get some sleep. What a day.

We woke up the next morning, got dressed and headed down to the dining room for a light breakfast. Our bathroom looked like something that you would see on *The Andy Griffith Show*. The sinks had two faucets: one for hot water and the other for cold. The whole bathroom was tiled (aqua blue) with one mirror and one closet containing an ironing board (with no iron) and a toilet plunger. The only air in the bathroom came from opening up the window and letting in a nice breeze. Since the hotel was small, the dining room only had seating for about six families. During our entire stay, we never saw another guest in that restaurant. The view from the restaurant was beautiful, and soon our spirits were lifted as we looked forward to meeting the children. We each ordered banana bread, fruit juice, and bottled water for breakfast.

When we finished, our driver was outside and waiting. We got into the van and were soon on our way. The trip to the Otters was like stepping back in time. Several roads were barely paved and we frequently ran across livestock in the middle of the road (we even saw bulls roaming very close to the road). The roads leading up to the hills above Kingstown were sharp and steep. There were no guardrails, and a few times, I was sure that we were about to drive right off the road. We passed several vehicles that I later learned were commuter buses. They were old Toyota vans (similar to one we were riding in) that were filled to capacity. These were private vehicles with drivers who were approved to carry passengers. More people meant more money so the drivers really packed them in. At one stop, I counted at least ten people who were already in the van and the driver was trying to get more in by yelling at people to make room for more. As we kept going, we saw fewer and fewer people. Close to town, we saw shopping areas that resembled strip shopping malls in the United States. As we went on, we saw more and more private homes that also doubled as the local grocery store. Closer to the Otters, we started seeing fewer grocery stores and more fruit and vegetable stands. We entered a charming little community, and pretty soon, we turned off of the paved road and started down a dirt driveway and then stopped in front of a house. The moment of truth had arrived.

CHAPTER 14
MEETING LEZROY AND NEILAH

When we got out of the van, the Otters came out to meet us, and there standing on the front porch were Lezroy and Neilah. They were both shy and didn't know what to expect so at first they kept their distance. I remember that Lezroy had on a Phoenix Suns basketball jersey and Neilah had a head full of hair. Before our arrival, we saw pictures and a few short videos of the children, but meeting them for the first time was an awesome experience. We greeted them, gave them a quick hug, and then headed inside. They didn't say much so we gave them a little space to give them time to figure things out. Julia went into the family room to get to know Lezroy and Neilah while we went into the kitchen for some small talk with the Otters.

Before leaving the United States, Penny told us that it is customary to bring a small gift to the foster family as a thank you for all of their work in caring for "our" children. After presenting the gift, we sat down to talk. Mr. Otter was jovial and always cracking jokes while Mrs. Otter was a little more reserved. We thanked them for inviting us into their home and engaged in a few pleasantries and talked about our trip. Before long, we headed to the family room so that we could get to know the children. We brought a few simple gifts (like Legos and other games), as well as some clothes that we knew they needed. We used the gifts as a way to break the ice. Soon, they were trying to figure out the games and started laughing and having a good time. The biggest thing that caught their eye was the technology that we brought along. We opened up our iPads and iPhones to show them pictures of our lives back home. They were intrigued and were interested in learning more.

After a few hours, Mrs. Otter called us to say that lunch was ready. It is customary for the foster family to host a perspective adoption family for lunch so that they may spend as much time as possible getting to know the child (or in our case, the children). Before we arrived, Penny told us about some of the common dishes that people on the island typically eat and asked if there were any restrictions to our diet. I tried to be nice and say that whatever they had was fine, but Renita was a bit more honest and told Penny that she was willing to try anything except for goat. When the Otters found out that we weren't a fan of goat meat, they were very surprised. On St. Vincent, goat meat is a delicacy and is served only on special occasions. Instead of goat, Mrs. Otter made a dish called *roti* (it was made out of ground chick peas that had been formed into some sort of pastry and filled with curried chicken and other local ingredients), fruits, vegetables, and some sort of homemade drinks (they had ginger, sea moss, water and something that had a milk-like consistency that I didn't recognize). The kids ate a huge amount of food and then went into the family room to play with their new toys. Julia ate her food (she

Discerning God's Purpose

CHAPTER 14

wanted to try the new food), and when she finished, went to join Lezroy and Neilah in the family room. We stayed behind to help clean up and to talk to the Otters about their experiences thus far with the children.

They told us about the environment that Lezroy and Neilah came from, their family background, and how they became available for adoption (it turns out that Mr. Otter knew their mom, and one day she approached him to ask for help since she knew that he was a foster parent). They said that the biggest issue that they had thus far was introducing structure and discipline to the children. Before they came, Lezroy and Neilah spent a lot of time on their own. Their mom would frequently leave them in an apartment alone while she went to work and sometimes neighbors would come down and give them food throughout the day. On the days when no one would come, Lezroy would cook ramen noodles as a meal for the two of them. They were both used to doing whatever they wanted, whenever they wanted, with no one to tell them no. After coming to the Otters, they both began to attend school on a regular basis (because of their Mom's work schedule, they previously would attend school sporadically). They showed us their grades and other school-related materials so that we would have an idea of where they were academically. Overall, the Otters felt that they would do well in a structured environment, but it would require time and patience.

After cleaning up and talking with the Otters, we went back to the family room to be with the children. We saw all three interacting well and noticed Lezroy and Neilah trying to use a little sign language with Julia. We brought some simple sign language books with us and saw that Julia started teaching a few signs to her new siblings. While we were observing the children, I saw someone enter the home. She came up to me and starting talking about how well the children seemed to be getting along. After a few minutes of small talk, she introduced herself. For the sake of privacy, I'll call her Mrs. Maxwell. She was the president of the adoption board for St. Vincent and stopped by to meet us and to see how the visit was going. We had been told to expect her, but her unannounced arrival still caught me by surprise. After a few more hours, it was time to go back to the hotel. We had a long day, and after a short and not very restful night, we were beyond tired.

We said our goodbyes then climbed back into the van for the trip back to town. Mrs. Maxwell didn't live too far away so our driver agreed to drop her off along the way. We all got in and started up the steep hill to get back to the main road. The driver tried a number of times but the van just didn't have enough power to make it up that steep hill with the five of us inside. Since she was in front, Mrs. Maxwell decided to get out and walk up the hill and then got back in when the van hit the main road. We dropped Mrs. Maxwell off at an intersection close to her home (the driver later told me that he does that all the time, and it was only a short walk up another hill to her home) and then continued our trip back to the hotel. Not wanting to have another ham and cheese sandwich, we asked the driver to stop along the way so that we could grab something to eat and take it back to the hotel. We happened upon a Pizza Hut, so we stopped in and ordered a pizza. While Pizza

Discerning God's Purpose

CHAPTER 14

Hut is an American restaurant chain, like most other franchises, this restaurant adapted to the tastes of its local clientele. We ordered a pepperoni pizza and when it was ready, we noticed that there was something different about the pizza. Instead of having cheese made from cow's milk, ours was made of goat's milk (much to Renita's dismay). Instead of pepperoni made from pork, ours was made of meat that came from local grass-fed cows. It was a little different but we were still able to enjoy a little slice of home.

When we got back to the hotel and entered our room, it felt like we were in Hades again. I turned on the air conditioning and prepared myself for a long wait while the room cooled down. There was a television in the room so we turned it on just to pass the time. There was only one television station on St. Vincent, however, the room did have cable TV, and the majority of the channels were from the United States. We were looking at a cable feed out of Miami. We were able to watch the news and then wind down for the night while watching ESPN. We got up the next day, and it was basically a repeat of what we did the day before. We were able to spend some more time with the kids until late afternoon when it was time for us to go. We promised to stay in touch with the Otters and to talk with Lezroy and Neilah on a weekly basis. After thanking the Otters for their hospitality, we said our goodbyes, climbed back into the van and were on our way. Our return to the hotel was uneventful, and we soon found ourselves back in our hot room (incidentally, that morning, I saw the person who serviced our room and asked why the air conditioner was always turned off after we left the room. She told us that it was hotel policy and that the owner required them to turn it off when no one was in the room in order to save electricity). So much for customer service. After another restless night, we got up early and headed to the airport for our trip home. We flew from St. Vincent to the island of Trinidad and Tobago and then on to Miami. I was never so happy to get back to the United States. After going through customs, the first thing that we did was grab a burger so that we could truly enjoy the taste of home. After that, we flew back to D.C. where we spent the night with my parents before returning home to Austin. We arrived home late on a Friday afternoon and used the weekend to recover. Julia took the time to complete most of her homework over the weekend, and by Monday, it was back to the grind.

While traveling home, we talked about our visit and pretty much made the decision to proceed with the adoption. Julia told us that she liked Lezroy and Neilah and wanted them as her new brother and sister. No surprise there. Renita and I were generally satisfied with the progress that the kids made while staying with the Otters, and considering the fact that they still had a long way to go, we felt that we would still be able to make a difference in their lives. We also felt that despite their circumstances, they were getting a good foundation upon which we could build, in order to turn them into productive citizens. Last but certainly not least, we felt that God was calling us to adopt these children. On Monday, we called Penny and let her know that we wanted to proceed with the adoption. We were ready to take the plunge.

Discerning God's Purpose

CHAPTER 15
IT'S OFFICIAL

Over the next eight months, I continued to commute between Austin and Maryland for work. On weekends at home, the little time that we had together was spent filling out paperwork, hosting home visits, having phone consultations with Penny, and trying to spend at least some quality time with Julia before it was time to get back on the road again. The immigration process was the most demanding. Since we would be adopting Lezroy and Neilah from outside the United States, we had to go through a lengthy process in order to bring them into the country. Once the adoption was finalized in St. Vincent, we would need to apply for immigration status at the U.S. Embassy in Barbados (the closest American Embassy to St. Vincent). Once the visas were issued, we could then travel to the United States. Upon landing in the United States and processing through customs, they would immediately become U.S. citizens. The two-step process required a mound of paperwork along with a great deal of patience. A few months after returning from St. Vincent, Penny told us that we received a favorable recommendation from the St. Vincent Adoption Board to adopt Lezroy and Neilah. Soon thereafter, we received preliminary approval from the Department of Homeland Security to bring Lezroy and Neilah into the country after the adoption was finalized. The only thing left was for the family court in Kingstown to grant final approval for the adoption to be official. Penny was well versed in the process and kept us informed about what would take place during the court hearing so we were very confident that this step was a mere formality. The law didn't require our presence in court so we chose to remain in the United States while being represented in court by our St. Vincent attorney. Thus far, everything proceeded according to the plan that Penny had previously outlined. Having no reason to worry, we continued with our plans to bring Lezroy and Neilah to their new home.

On the day of the court hearing, we waited for Penny to call us with news that the adoption was now official. Penny told us that our case would be one of the first on the court docket and that we should expect a call no later than around noon. Well, noon came and went with no call. One o'clock came, still no call. Two o'clock came, nothing. Three o'clock, same thing. We were starting to get concerned. Finally just before four o'clock, Penny called. Since Renita was in Austin and I was in D.C., we conferenced her in so that we could both hear everything at the same time. After exchanging some quick pleasantries, she told us that things had not quite gone according to plan. The presiding judge was new to family court and was looking to assert her authority in this case. She didn't want to simply approve the adoption based on the board's recommendation but wanted to determine for herself if this adoption should go through. The judge questioned the birth mother in court to ensure she knew that she would be permanently giving up

CHAPTER 15

her parental rights. After that, she questioned Lezroy and Neilah to see for herself that they both understood what was happening and were willing to go to America to live with a new family. She went through all of the adoption paperwork but before granting final approval, she wanted us to return to the island and appear in her court so that she could make a suitability determination for herself. At that point, our attorney had enough and went to bat for us. He explained to the judge that all of the due diligence had already taken place. He also said that we had already made one trip to St. Vincent to meet with the children and the president of the adoption board prior to the board's recommendation.

He went on to explain the adoption timeline up to this point (we had been involved in this process for seventeen months), the costs that had already been incurred, the upcoming carnival celebration on the island and how that would significantly affect the timeframe for us to appear in court (flights and hotels on the island were extremely limited and another hearing would push the timeframe out at least another three months). Above all, what she was requesting wasn't legally required for the adoption to be finalized. Lastly, he reminded the judge of the undue hardship that her decision would have on the adoption board as well as the Otters because of the limited resources available from the government of St. Vincent to continue to care for Lezroy and Neilah while in foster care. Our attorney reminded the judge that Lezroy and Neilah were ten and nine, respectively, and older children are typically harder to place.

Although we never said this, our attorney stated that any delay could possibly jeopardize the adoption with the children being the ultimate victims. Based on all of these facts, the judge decided to go ahead and grant final approval. After going through all of that, Penny finally said, "Congratulations, you are now legally the parents of Lezroy and Neilah." We hung up with Penny, and I got back on the phone with Renita. I could hear the emotion in her voice. This journey hadn't been easy, but we followed the path that we were led. Lezroy and Neilah were finally ours.

Next, I called my parents who were of course overjoyed with the news. They had followed the ups and downs of this journey and were happy that this part of the roller-coaster ride was over. When I hung up with my parents, I thought of my father-in-law. He had passed away a few years prior, but oh how I wished that he were still alive to enjoy this moment. After a moment of reflection, I got back to work. I had much to plan for now that a new journey was about to begin.

That night after work, I stopped by to check on my mother-in-law and to share the good news. It was a bittersweet moment. For the past six years, she lived in an assisted living facility after being formally diagnosed with Alzheimer's disease. Since my father-in-law passed away, her condition had steadily declined to where she was now barely able to speak. I don't know if she understood a word I said that night, but at least I saw a smile on her face.

Once the adoption was finalized, by law we had to wait thirty days to go and pick up the children. Based on what happened at the court hearing, we had no intention of testing the limits of that

Discerning God's Purpose

CHAPTER 15

law. Penny had previously told us that we needed to return to St. Vincent for a few days in order to pick up the children and to finalize the adoption documents. We asked why it would take so long, and Penny said that it was mainly due to our attorney's schedule. She also said that we could use the time to get to know the children while in an environment that was familiar to them. While that would be nice, after our last trip, I had no desire to return to the island. Besides, since Renita's mom was so sick due to complications from Alzheimer's disease, we wanted to limit our travel as much as possible. Having already made hotel reservations in Barbados for the time necessary to complete the immigration process, we asked Penny if it was possible for us to meet the children there. She checked into it and told us that Mrs. Maxwell would be happy to escort the children to Barbados and we could sign the required documents and take custody there. We agreed on an escort fee for Mrs. Maxwell and to pick up the travel costs, but to us, it was money well spent. We later found out that she had a daughter who lived in Barbados so for her, it was a nice way for her to see her daughter for free. In the end, everyone was happy. Now, the only thing left was for Penny to collect her final fee, for us to make flight reservations, pack enough clothes for our new family, and to be on our way.

Three weeks later, we traveled to Barbados to take custody of our new children. The trip started with an interesting twist. We decided to drive from Austin to Houston and then fly from there to Miami and then on to Barbados. Houston is a three-hour drive from Austin so before leaving for the airport, we checked with the airline that morning and confirmed that our flight was still scheduled to leave on time. When we arrived at the airport in Houston, we found out that there had been a mechanical issue with the plane that was going to delay our departure for over two hours. Because of the delay, we would miss our connecting flight in Miami to Barbados. The airline only had one flight per day to Barbados, so we would need to stay in Miami overnight and catch a flight the next day. I was ticked because had the airline let us known earlier, we could have stayed at home for an additional day. What really got me mad was when I asked the airline agent to rebook our entire travel for the next day; he said that he would be happy to but that the airline would charge me a rebooking fee. When I started to protest, he said that there was nothing that he could do; however, he said that because the issue was the airline's fault, by keeping the same itinerary, there would be no fee and the airline would give us hotel and food vouchers for our stay in Miami. Since I wasn't willing to pay $600 for something that wasn't our fault, we accepted the vouchers and spent the night in Miami. We also called the hotel in Barbados to let them know what was going on so we wouldn't lose our reservation. With that done, we had no choice but to settle down and wait.

We spent the night in Miami, got on the plane to Barbados and made it without further incident. I booked us into a nice resort property in Barbados where we could relax and be in somewhat of a comfortable environment while we got acquainted with the children and waited to complete the immigration process before returning home. Most hotels have a policy of charging you for one

CHAPTER 15

night's stay if you cancel (or in our case a last-minute change) a reservation well in advance. Some will even agree to waive the fee if the reason for the cancellation was something out of your control (like an aircraft maintenance issue). The hotel had a 72-hour cancellation policy, so upon our arrival, the front desk clerk informed me that I would still be charged for the previous day. *Here we go again*, I thought. I asked to talk to the manager. I explained that I was a long-time member of that hotel brand's rewards program, explained what happened with the airline, and asked if an exception could be made (after all, I was still staying for six nights so I was still providing him with revenue). He said that the policy couldn't be changed so he was required to charge me for the night; however, with my status as a rewards member (and other discounts for being a government employee), I negotiated an upgrade to a much larger room for the same amount that I would have paid in the first place. In the end, we were able to make the best of what was starting to be a bad situation. After checking in, we went to our room to relax for a few hours until it was time to return to the airport to collect the children.

As was the case on St. Vincent, Penny had arranged for a driver to be assigned to us for the duration of our stay in Barbados. The driver she recommended (David) was a retired member of the Barbados Defense Force, and as a former member of the military myself, we had an instant bond. He had worked with Penny for many years and knew where we needed to go so he was able to recommend a schedule that allowed us to do what we needed to do with minimum delay. He also offered to take us on a tour of the island while waiting for the immigration documents to be completed. Best of all, David was always on time so we never had to worry about any missed appointments. We couldn't have been more pleased with Penny's recommendation or with the service that David provided. At the appointed time, David picked us up at the hotel and brought us to the airport to meet Mrs. Maxwell and the children. They would be traveling on the same airline that we used before, so we were prepared for the "island time" delay. This particular flight wasn't too bad since it would now arrive only an hour late (the best explanation of island time that I have heard actually came from the comedian Gabriel Iglesias when he said, "we get there when we get there"). By this point, we waited about eighteen months to complete the adoption process so we could wait an additional hour for the plane. David recommended a place for us to eat while we waited, so we were able to try some of the local delicacies. Finally, it was time. The flight had landed so we gathered just outside of the door that they would be coming through and tried to contain our excitement. After what seemed like a long time, finally we saw some of the passengers start to come out and then saw Mrs. Maxwell and the children come through the door. We rushed over, greeted them with hugs and kisses, took pictures and videos of the arrival and then moved to a nearby table to sign and collect the required documents. After everything was signed, we formally gained custody of the children. Lezroy and Neilah were naturally apprehensive. Other than spending a few hours together in the Otters' home on St. Vincent and spending a

Discerning God's Purpose

CHAPTER 15

few minutes on weekly phone calls, they really didn't know anything about us. They were naturally wary and mostly stuck to themselves. After saying our goodbyes to Mrs. Maxwell, we got in David's van and headed back to the hotel.

CHAPTER 16
A NEW PURPOSE

Before traveling to Barbados, Renita and I dreamed of having a nice vacation with our new expanded family where we could spend a few days getting reacquainted with Lezroy and Neilah in a relaxed atmosphere. That was not to be. Kids being kids, Lezroy and Neilah decided to test us the first night. After dinner, Renita was talking to all three kids about behavior when Lezroy suddenly walked out of the room. We knew from our prior discussions with Penny that St. Vincent was a male-dominated society with a lack of respect for women. Apparently, Lezroy thought that he didn't have to listen to Renita, so he left the room. Big mistake. The look on Renita's face reminded me of an old western movie where there was a shootout at the OK Corral. I didn't say anything but just moved out of the way. I knew that she needed to establish right then and there that there were two parents who were to be respected in our house. Renita went into the room where Lezroy was, grabbed him by the collar and marched his butt back where we were all standing. At the time, Lezroy was less than five feet tall and weighed less than ninety pounds. She was taller and bigger than he was so she got right in his face and told him in no uncertain terms that he was to listen and respect her while she was

CHAPTER 16

talking. The look on his face was priceless. It was obvious that no woman had ever done that to him before. It also served as a taste of what was yet to come.

Not wanting to be outdone, the next day Neilah decided to go after me. We decided to have lunch at one of the restaurants inside the hotel. We all looked at the menu, and Neilah ordered a sausage pizza for lunch. When it arrived, it was different from what she expected. Apparently on St. Vincent, "sausage" is sliced and looks like what Americans refer to as pepperoni. Renita, Julia, and I had ordered the pepperoni pizza and when she saw what we had, Neilah threw a fit. She began to throw a temper tantrum, kept saying that "Me no like!" the pizza and refused to eat. The waiter tried to make Neilah happy by offering to take her pizza back and exchange it for something else, but I was not having it. Her attitude was unacceptable, and she was not going to pout her way into getting what she wanted. I told her that she ordered the pizza and was going to either eat that pizza or nothing at all. In response, Neilah slammed her hand on the table and shoved the plate away, almost dropping it on the floor in the process. When that happened, something in the back of my mind said "Are you ready? Let's get it on." I heard the fight bell ring in my head as I hauled her behind out of the restaurant to have a "nice" chat. This is probably a good time to admit that while I am a Christian, I am not perfect. There are times when I still struggle with a cursing spirit, and this was shaping up to be one of those times. I wanted to use some nice four-letter words, but I did my best to remember that this was a nine-year-old girl, who only a few days before had said goodbye to everyone and everything that she had ever known. She was also trying to adjust to a new family and besides, I was supposed to be a stabilizing figure and one of the adults in the family. Reluctantly, I refrained. Still, it was on like popcorn.

We knew from the Otters that Neilah would cry when she didn't get her way. Many times, people would either give her what she wanted or would simply leave her alone. Not today. When we got to a quiet area, I told her in no uncertain terms that that she was nine and not two and in this family, she would not act this way. I also warned her of the dire consequences that would happen if she continued with her present behavior. She didn't look all that convinced, but her behavior improved. When we returned to the table, Neilah was calm but again refused to eat the pizza. I had enough.

"Fine" I said. "Lunch was over. If you won't eat the pizza, then you won't eat." She pouted but left the restaurant in silence. I was a little embarrassed by what happened, but I didn't care. We were setting the tone for behavior expectations, and if I needed to get a little loud in a restaurant, so be it. As someone once told me, embarrassment doesn't kill you. It only stings for a little while and then it goes away.

Not satisfied with the reaction that she got from me, a little later, Neilah tried the same tactic with Renita and got a similar response. We were scheduled to take the children to a kids' play area at the hotel for them to have a little fun and to play some games but because of her behavior with me earlier, Neilah wasn't allowed to go and have fun. Renita was a little tired, so she decided to stay

Discerning God's Purpose

CHAPTER 16

in the room with Neilah while I took Lezroy and Julia down to play. We had just left the room when Neilah decided to throw a tantrum. Renita had that old familiar song come into her head, "I'm about to whip somebody's a$@" but like me, she refrained. There is, however, something special about a woman-to-girl discussion that can scare the daylights out of a kid. When we came back to the room, Neilah was sniffling and had a little attitude on her face but was none the worse for wear. Renita said that she didn't touch her (whew) but let her know that her attitude was not acceptable. Neilah still wasn't through. Over the next few days, we saw that this was a familiar pattern with Neilah. If there was something that she didn't like or didn't want to do, she simply started to cry and throw a tantrum. Each time, she was met with the same response.

On the day before we left the island, we took a tour of the island with our driver David. After a little while, Neilah grew bored and didn't want to continue with the tour so she started crying. This time it was my turn. We ended up stopping at a local mall to pick up some souvenirs for our family back home. While Renita, Lezroy, and Julia went in, Neilah and I stayed out in the van with David. Again, I told her that her behavior was unacceptable. I guess Neilah wanted to show me that she was the boss so she threw the biggest tantrum that she could. She cried harder, stomped her feet, slapped at the windows, let drool hang from her mouth and did everything that she could to attract attention to herself and to me. I guess she thought that I would be embarrassed and would give in to her demands. Not so. My response never changed. I told her that I expected more out of a nine year old and started taking privileges away. I also told her that she was going to clean up the mess that she made in the van and was going to apologize to David for her behavior. She screamed, cried, hit the back of the seat and threw her tantrum for an additional thirty minutes. I asked David to go inside the mall and tell Renita that we would be staying right where we were (in the warm van) until Neilah's behavior improved. Finally, Neilah got the message that her tantrum wasn't working and got herself together. I got out some tissues and had her clean up her face and then clean up the mess she made and apologize to David. When everything was back to normal, Renita came out of the mall with Julia and Lezroy, and we continued our tour. We didn't take a hard line because we wanted to be mean and nasty to Lezroy and Neilah. We knew that they were testing us, and we had to establish the ground rules regarding expectations in our family. We knew that structure was something that they didn't have and we knew that was one of the things that they needed. Lastly, we knew that no one expected anything of Lezroy and Neilah before, but we wanted to show them that not only did we think that they could do better, we expected it. As our time in Barbados drew to a close, their attitudes did start to improve. We received immigration approval for Lezroy and Neilah to travel to the United States. We packed our bags, said goodbye to Barbados and boarded our plane to Miami. We thought that we were finished with the disciplinary issues and that Lezroy and Neilah were ready to become members of the family. Little did we know that our challenges were only just beginning.

Discerning God's Purpose

CHAPTER 16

Our trip back to Austin was uneventful. I took six weeks of leave from work so that I would have enough time not only to pick up the kids from Barbados but to try to form a relationship with Lezroy and Neilah before having to get back on the road. We got home and settled into a new routine. We introduced them to our friends and extended family and tried to make them feel at home. At the same time, we also made it clear that we were no longer on vacation and that there were certain expectations of everyone living in the house. We all had assigned responsibilities, including caring for our family pet. Lezroy and Neilah were still wary of us but seeing as they really had no choice, went about learning what was expected of them. We showed them that we had the same expectations of them that we had of our older daughter Julia. We were also now a family, and even though we knew that it would take time, we had to learn to trust one another. Before the adoption, Lezroy and Neilah both had an initial psychological screening that concluded both were physically and emotionally stable. Since Lezroy and Neilah had undergone a massive change in their family situation, we knew that counseling might at some point prove useful. In the beginning, however, we wanted to see what we could do on our own without involving outside help. This decision would prove to test the limits of our family bond.

Lezroy and Neilah were older at the time of their adoption so much of their character makeup had been established on St. Vincent. Unfortunately, we had the job of trying to break bad habits in order to establish more healthy ones. Lezroy, especially, didn't like to listen when we tried to give him advice on how to do something. He told me early on that there was nothing that we could teach him so his first instincts were to try to figure things out for himself. This first became a problem when dealing with the family pet. We have a small dog (a tea cup Yorkshire terrier) named Emmy. Emmy has the perfect temperament for Julia as she is very friendly and likes people. Although she is small and only weighs a little over three pounds, a dog is still a dog. If you don't treat dogs a certain way, they will certainly let you know about their unhappiness. I guess Lezroy didn't like the fact that he was required to share in the responsibility of taking care of Emmy. He would have to take Emmy out into the backyard so that she could do her business. Afterwards, he had to clean up after her (including bagging her little "packages"), play with her for a few minutes, and then fill her bowls with food and water. It is a process that usually takes about a half hour and is a shared responsibility among the family. Early one morning, I got up to check on Emmy's supplies and noticed that the handle on her leash was broken. We had the leash for four years and had no problems, but now, after only a week with Lezroy and Neilah in the house, it was broken. Before I could say anything, Lezroy came downstairs to take Emmy for her morning walk. He went to grab Emmy to put the leash on her when suddenly she began snapping at him. Over and over again, he would put his hand in the crate to grab the dog, and each time she would snap at him.

He looked at me and started crying, saying that he was afraid of Emmy and wanted me to take her for a walk. I was immediately suspicious and decided to use this to teach him a lesson. I asked

CHAPTER 16

him what he did to Emmy. Of course, he said nothing. I told him that dogs are very predictable. If you are kind to a dog, the dog is kind in return; however, if you are mean to a dog, they return that favor as well. I told him that Emmy had been a part of the family for over four years, and in all that time, she had never snapped at any of us. She was trained and had a good temperament. Now, all of a sudden there was a problem. So I asked him again, what did he do to the dog. Again, he said nothing and again started his little crying game.

Well, it was time for him to get his first lesson in personal responsibility. Lezroy, like any boy his age, had a deep affinity for food and large quantities of it. He especially had an affinity for bacon which ironically is what we planned to have for breakfast. I told him that it was his responsibility to walk the dog so he needed to solve the problem with Emmy before he ate his breakfast. The look on his face was priceless. I was holding him accountable for his actions and making him responsible for solving this particular problem. I offered to give him tips on the easiest ways to pick Emmy up from behind so that he could put the leash on without her snapping at him, but I wouldn't do it for him. He still insisted on doing it his way. I said fine and told the rest of the family what happened and how Lezroy was responsible for solving his problem. No one was allowed to solve it for him. With that, I went into the kitchen to cook breakfast.

Time and again he tried to do it his way, and every time, Emmy snapped at him. I remember growing up, I sometimes had a stubborn streak and I remember my Mom saying that a hard head leads to a soft behind. I wasn't planning on spanking him, but I decided to let Emmy teach him this particular lesson about the Golden Rule (do unto others what you would have done to you). We kept an eye on him to make sure that he didn't get hurt, but he was learning the consequences for his actions. Every time Emmy snapped at him, he would use his crying game to get someone to feel sorry for him or would ask one of us to do it for him. I said no. He was ten years old (soon to be eleven) and needed to be responsible for his actions. I also said that if he didn't do anything, like he was claiming, he had no reason to be afraid of a three-pound dog.

When breakfast was ready, he tried to come into the kitchen to sit down and eat, but I reminded him of the rules. He had to take care of Emmy first, and then he could sit down and eat. He was stubborn (just like the Otters told us), but I wouldn't budge. The rest of us finished eating and cleaned up the kitchen while he continued to try to put the leash on Emmy. Again and again he tried with the same result. Morning turned into afternoon. He cried again and again, but I wouldn't budge. His sisters even tried to tell him how to do it, but he only wanted to do it his way. Finally, around four o'clock that afternoon, I guess his stomach couldn't take it anymore, so Lezroy finally asked me for help. I talked him through how to re-establish a relationship with the dog and how to put the leash on Emmy. This time, Emmy didn't snap at him, and he was finally able to take her for a walk.

Afterward, I told him that because of his attitude, he let a five- minute issue turn into a seven-hour problem. When I asked

Discerning God's Purpose

CHAPTER 16

him why he refused to ask for help, he said that he thought that I wanted Emmy to bite him so he didn't want my help. I asked him if he had eaten food at our house since he had been living with us. He chuckled a little and said yes. I asked if he had gotten sick from any of the food and he said no. Then I said "Oh, so we didn't put anything in your food to make you sick, huh? If I really wanted to hurt you, it is much easier to put something in your food than to have Emmy bite you." I told him that the biggest lesson here was that he has to learn how and when to trust people. I reminded him that we are his family now, and like it or not, he had to trust us. I also told him that just like with Emmy, he needed to work to establish a relationship with the family so that there could be a level of trust between all of us. I don't know if it stuck, but at least he got a real lesson in trust.

During the initial few months of their stay, it was clear that Lezroy and Neilah were still determined to do things their way. Before school started, we wanted them to get into the habit of reading so we required them to read for thirty minutes each day (including Saturdays and Sundays). They had trouble with language, and this was one of the best ways that we knew of to increase their vocabulary and to get into the habit of learning new things. We asked them to both read aloud, but it was very clear early on neither wanted to do it and were just going through the motions. Lezroy thought that he already could read well and didn't need any improvement. When I asked questions about the story that he just read, he couldn't answer them so I had him read the story again. Neilah, on the other hand, was very apprehensive about reading. We knew from the Otters that she had great difficulty in reading. She didn't want to read, but we gave her books at the beginner level and sat with her while she read. When she would get to a word that she didn't know or understand how to pronounce, she would try to skip it. When we insisted that she sound out the word, she would get frustrated and cry, expecting us to give up and leave her alone, just like others did when she was back in St. Vincent. Nope, not this time. We pushed her to sound out words and to continue until her thirty minutes were complete. As time went on, we did start to see some improvements. Both still struggled with reading, but we only wanted them to try and do their best. We kept requiring them to read each day until it was time for school to begin.

Since St. Vincent is not known for having an advanced educational system, and both missed significant school time during the past few years and had birthdays that fell in the last quarter of the year, the school recommended that Lezroy and Neilah repeat the grade that they had just completed in St. Vincent. Lezroy would begin school in the fifth grade and Neilah the 4th. Since he would be repeating the fifth grade, Lezroy thought that this would be an easy year for him and started to relax. When school started, he thought that he would show off his reading skills by volunteering to read in front of the class. Neilah, on the other hand, was just the opposite. She tried to be cute and nice to her teacher in the beginning but then sat in the back of the class and hoped that she wouldn't be called on to read in front of the class. Both received a wakeup call in a hurry. As part of their initial assessment, both

Discerning God's Purpose

were required to take a reading test and scored well below grade level. Neilah's teacher recommended that she be placed in the English as a second language (ESL) program. We readily agreed and then requested the same for Lezroy. Both would receive the additional instruction as a way to improve their comprehension as well as their language. Suddenly, the school year wasn't looking so easy for Lezroy.

At the beginning of the year, teachers also gave students a preliminary assessment test in reading, math, and science to identify areas that a student needs to improve in before taking the statewide standardized assessment tests that are required each spring. Since neither had much experience with taking standardized tests in St. Vincent, their teachers also recommended that Lezroy and Neilah receive extra tutoring on test-taking skills to give them strategies to help them pass the tests. For Lezroy, this tutoring was very important since it was a key factor in being promoted to middle school. The tests showed that he was going to have to work hard in order to pass both tests and be promoted to the sixth grade. The good news was that Lezroy's teacher noticed two things that would help him pass the tests. First, he was very competitive. He wanted to win no matter what. Whether it was being first in line, first to finish his food, or first to finish a test, he always wanted to be first. Second, Renita and I have always been very involved parents and that, coupled with the fact that he had great teachers who really took an interest in him, greatly enhanced his chance for success.

We also had a third and important secret weapon. As I said before, St. Vincent is a male-dominated society (very chauvinistic in their ways). Lezroy had been exposed to that culture so he never wanted to lose, especially to a girl. Well, our (now) oldest daughter, Julia was an honor roll student. When the first grade reports came in, Julia's grades were higher than his and by a wide margin. I must admit, I took the opportunity to stoke the fire. I would repeatedly say, "You mean to tell me that you are letting a girl show you up? I thought that you said that you wanted to be the best. I thought that you said that you didn't like to lose. Julia is beating you like a drum. She even has additional challenges that make it harder for her but she is still beating you like a chump." On and on I went, challenging his "manhood" about letting a girl beat him. If he was doing his best, I never would have said a word, but it was obvious that he was only doing enough to barely get by. By teasing him like this, I was also letting him know that anything less than his best was unacceptable. I kept after him. Eventually, the more I teased, the madder he got. Soon, he started studying like crazy. Pretty soon his grades started coming up. He would spend extra time with his teachers trying to understand assignments, and in general get up to speed on what was going on.

One of the problems that we identified early on is that no one ever cared enough about Lezroy or Neilah to hold them to high standards. No one expected anything out of them so they were just allowed to slide by. In St. Vincent, his grades were 50s and 60s, and since no one said anything, he thought that these grades were

Discerning God's Purpose

acceptable. Renita and I made it clear that we had much higher expectations.

The other issue was stubbornness. We first noticed it when Lezroy had an issue with Emmy, and we were seeing it again when it came to schoolwork. When they came home and Renita or I would ask how their day was, Lezroy and Neilah would always say that things were fine, but then we started getting notices about missed assignments or a bad grade on a test. When we asked why they hadn't said anything, Lezroy would say that he wanted to do it on his own. On the other hand, if Neilah needed help, she would only go and ask Lezroy. Then there was still the issue of trust. They were both very secretive and would try to hide things or would lie about completing the most basic of tasks.

The family was divided into two "camps" with Julia, Renita, and I on one side and Lezroy and Neilah on the other. It became apparent that the underlying issue was still one of trust. We kept hearing from teachers, church leaders, neighbors, and others how pleasant and respectful Lezroy and Neilah were, but when it came to us, we saw a different side entirely. The key issue was that they really didn't see us as parents but as a source for providing them with the essentials of food, clothing, and shelter. We soon realized that no amount of punishment was going to force them to change their attitude or to care about us in the same way that they cared for each other. No, if they were going to change, they were going to have to want to do it for themselves. For this, I knew that I needed to seek a higher power.

During the adoption period, God clearly revealed to me that Lezroy and Neilah belonged in our family. Now, in the middle of this storm, I wasn't so sure. We sought advice from friends and counseling professionals, but the common question that kept coming up was "Can you send them back?" The answer is *of course not*. We knew that they were supposed to stay with us and we needed to make it work but the big question was how? The only way to answer this question was to again seek wisdom from the one who knows all. I began to pray for wisdom. At first, I thought that Lezroy and Neilah were sent to us to help Julia. After they arrived and Julia took on the role of big sister, we saw Julia grow and mature before our eyes to become a more confident and responsible young lady. She became more diligent in her schoolwork and even tried to set a better example as their big sister. She started teaching them sign language, talked to them about how to do well in their new environment, and in general tried to show love, but, like the two of us, soon became frustrated with the actions of Lezroy and Neilah.

She still wanted them as siblings and wanted to help, but instead of telling them what to do, she decided to show them. While still focused on high school, she began thinking about what would come next. We always had high expectations for her and after moving to Texas and keeping up with her peers, she developed high expectations for herself. She became interested in helping people and became interested in the field of law and advocacy. She wanted to enjoy her final years of high school but knew that colleges looked for well-rounded students when considering applicants

Discerning God's Purpose

CHAPTER 16

for admission. Despite the physical challenges associated with CP, along with her studies, she got involved with extra-curricular activities like robotics, tech clubs, drama, and cheerleading. She didn't talk the talk but walked the walk.

Gradually, I started noticing Lezroy and Neilah beginning to pay attention and mimic the things that Julia was doing. God was showing me that although I needed to continue to hold Lezroy and Neilah to the expectation of being good citizens, he was also using Julia to teach them that they could find their own way to do it. Sometimes, I simply needed to take a step back and let God take the lead.

To illustrate this point, I thought back to a funny story that I heard about when I was younger. A young kid was learning about U.S. history in school. One day the teacher asked her students to name a patriotic American. Most kids mentioned one of the founding fathers or a U.S. president. This kid, being the class clown, thought about a show he had seen recently on television and mentioned the name of Redd Foxx. The teacher said "Redd Foxx, the comedian? Why would you say that?" The boy said "Simple. His name is Redd, his hair is white, and his material is blue." After the laughter from the other kids died down, he went on to talk about the work that Redd Foxx and others did to open up jobs in television to women and people of color. While his answer was unique and may have started out as a joke, he soon turned serious and proceeded to give a thoughtful answer for which he received an A. He found his own way. I thought if it worked for that kid, maybe it could work for Lezroy and Neilah.

I believe that Renita and I are good parents, but like anyone else, we can occasionally make mistakes. When Julia, Lezroy, or Neilah did something that we didn't think was appropriate, respectful, or they handled a situation differently from our way of thinking, we could be quick to correct them. With Julia, things were and are a bit easier because she has been with us her whole life and knows of our expectations. We had a chance to mold her character from the time she was an infant so she has values and characteristics that are similar to ours. She has her own personality and at times can be very stubborn, but has a fierce work ethic and has a tender heart of gold. We have grown to develop a great relationship that is based on mutual trust and respect. Since Lezroy and Neilah had only been with us a short while, we are still working to establish the same type of relationship. They grew up in an unstructured environment for most of their young lives, so we tried our best to provide structure and a level of discipline in order to make them responsible citizens. At the same time, we wanted to show them love and to give them a sense of belonging. We did all kinds of activities as a family like playing games, going out to movies, going for walks, or just having a good time at home. We supported them when they wanted to talk about their mom or life back in St. Vincent. We celebrated their successes but were also there to console and encourage them when things didn't go their way.

Still, life in our house at times could still be very interesting. Lezroy could still be stubborn, and Neilah would sometimes get upset when she didn't get her way. As a family, we are still a

Discerning God's Purpose

CHAPTER 16

work in progress but the key is that we are making progress. I'm human. I can still get frustrated with any one of my children but it is during those times that God finds a way to let me know that I am not alone and to remind me of my purpose.

Earlier this year, my family and I were led to join a new church. Our old church was Bible-based and the pastor was (and is) a great man of God; however, we were led to switch because of a larger deaf ministry and a desire to serve His Kingdom in a different way. One of the first people that I met at the new church was a man named Gary. His wife was one of the leaders of the deaf ministry and they were also Elders at the church. Our families had a lot in common. His family relocated to Texas from the east coast (as did we), and their children attended the same school as Julia. They had also gone through the international adoption process and therefore were facing similar issues as we were. Renita spent time with Gary's wife Lisa and Tracy (the other leader of the deaf ministry) so Gary and I decided to meet for coffee and get to know each other a little better. We just hit it off and became fast friends. One coffee meeting, turned into another, and pretty soon we were meeting on a regular basis. We would talk about what God was doing in our lives and just take time out to encourage one another. Since he had adopted his kids a few years earlier than we did, I began to pick his brain about his experiences and how he handled things. When Lezroy or Neilah would make a mistake, I have a tendency to step in and try to "fix" the problem right away. One of the key pieces of advice that Gary gave me early on was to remind me that sometimes I need to step back and allow God to show them the way. He said that as long as I tried to "fix" things myself, God would step back and let me handle it, and most of the time, I would end up with a mess. On the other hand, if I called on Him for help, He would always be by my side. Our coffee sessions sometime reminded me of a therapy session, but ultimately, Gary not only helped me through one of the darkest periods of my life as a parent, but would help me re-discover my purpose.

During one of our conversations, I talked about how I was getting too old to deal with young children and the drama that pre-teens typically have. Gary reminded me that God doesn't make mistakes and that He always provides for our needs. I was able to think back to other times when I thought that I couldn't handle a situation or problem but that when I really needed it, a solution would appear as if by divine intervention. I thought about what Gary said and realized that God did indeed have a plan for my life, and that plan included Lezroy and Neilah. Even though they were born in another country and through another womb, Lezroy and Neilah are as much our children as Julia is and in God's eyes, we are responsible for preparing them for their assignment just as we are for Julia. I realized that we are the family that they need and are the key to unlocking their true potential. What I initially thought of as a curse will turn out to be one of my greatest blessings.

Part of our role in preparing them for their assignment is to lead them to the Father. They did attend church back in St. Vincent and even knew a few gospel songs, but they truly didn't know about God. Not only did our new church have a great message for

Discerning God's Purpose

adults, but they also had a great program for children as well. Our job was not to preach to them but just to get them to church and God would take it from there. After service, we normally ask about what they learned during their service. Initially, Lezroy would talk about the food that he ate and Neilah would talk about the toys that she received, but over time, they started paying attention and were able to tell us exactly what they learned. They even started talking about ways that they could apply the lessons in everyday life. We were starting to see a glimmer of hope. We started to see Lezroy and Neilah take responsibility for things like homework and chores without us asking. They still backslide and mess-up on occasion, like any other kid, but still, there is that glimmer of hope. Two steps forward and one step back still is a sign of progress. With God, all things are truly possible.

A NEW CALLING

Jeremiah 29:11 (NIV) says "For I know the plans I have for you," declares the LORD, "plans to prosper you and not to harm you, plans to give you hope and a future." Sometimes God closes doors for a reason. You may look at it as a setback, but really God is closing that door as a set-up for you to do something better. The key is to embrace God's will and to follow the plan that He has for you.

In college, I majored in business because that is where I believed I could earn a comfortable living for me and my family. For twenty-eight years I followed that path and, by most accounts, had a successful career. When we moved to Austin, however, I started seeing God begin to close the door on that career. I must admit that like Lezroy, I wanted to do things my way. I tried to keep the door open by continuing to travel across country on a weekly basis in order to keep my employer happy. When it became evident that I was not fulfilling my purpose because of my extended travel, I tried to find a similar job closer to home without any luck. For almost four years, I was stubborn and continued to try to do things my way by using any means necessary to keep that door open and to continue with my chosen career. That's when God stepped back and allowed all kinds of storms to come into my life.

He allowed relationships to be strained, bad financial breaks, and health issues to affect my life. Eventually, He broke me. I knew it was time to yield to the will of the Father.

I knew that things needed to change but at almost fifty years old, I didn't know what else I could do. That's when I discovered the passage of Isaiah 42:16 which states "And I will lead the blind in a way that they do not know, in paths that they have not known I will guide them. I will turn the darkness before them into light, the rough places into level ground. These are the things I do, and I do not forsake them." At that moment, I knew that I would be just fine as long as I put my trust in Him. When I made the decision to do that, God opened up my eyes and I began to think of things that before I never thought were possible. I asked God to order my steps so that I could follow His path and I haven't looked back. From that day forward, I have had a new calling in life, not just to focus on my own needs but to help others. In doing so, God began to use my gifts and talents in ways to help others as never before. When I focused on helping others, I realized that I was really helping myself.

CHAPTER 17
REVENGE

I enjoyed working for the federal government. I progressed in my career and had reached the level of a senior manager with a government agency. Nonetheless, I always believed that family came first. When it was time to finalize the adoption for Lezroy and Neilah, I didn't hesitate to take six weeks of paternity leave from work to spend time with my new expanded family. Many people think of the importance of Moms spending time with their new children, but it is just as important for Dads to have that time as well. I didn't want to bring the kids home one week and then be back on the road for work the next. I was, however, still a responsible manager so before I left, I made sure that the person who replaced me was fully informed and could make decisions on my behalf during my absence. While I had full faith and trust in my replacement, apparently my boss did not.

Although I was entitled to paternity leave under the Family and Medical Leave Act, my boss still asked if I would be willing to work remotely for a day or two a week during my time away. I am a people pleaser by nature so if it would help if I were available to answer questions or to give guidance to my replacement if needed, I was happy to oblige. Before agreeing to the request, I asked if the senior executive who had cancelled my telework agreement before would support this new request. My boss assured me that he would. Still, I wanted to get this new agreement in writing. I negotiated an agreement where I would be able to telework two days a week for up to a year after my paternity leave had ended. The request was approved by my boss as well as the Office of Human Resources (HR), and so after picking up the kids and returning to the United States, I began teleworking two days a week while still on paternity leave.

After returning to work full time, my boss suddenly had a change of heart and wanted to cancel the agreement. When I reminded her that the agreement had been approved not only by management but by HR as well, she agreed to drop the request. Not long afterwards, I began hearing rumors again about how management was unhappy with my telework agreement. *Here we go again,* I thought. This time, instead of making an appointment to see the same senior executive as before, I decided to wait to see if things would blow over. It didn't take long before I had my answer. Two months after I returned to work, I received an email from my second-line manager telling me that she was canceling my new telework agreement. She said that my absences were causing a performance issue and that was the reason for terminating the agreement. No examples cited and no warning, just an allegation of substandard performance. Now that got my attention. I had just received my annual performance evaluation after returning from paternity leave and I received an outstanding evaluation. I also never received any word from my manager since returning of any instances of poor performance. Now, less than two months later I was told that my performance was slipping. This was a hit job, and there was no way that I was going to let this stand. It was time to fight.

I replied to the email and requested that my second-line manager reconsider her decision based on some additional facts: my latest performance appraisal, recent examples of my effectiveness at work, and a desire to create a winning solution for the organization as well as myself. I including an offer to change my area of responsibilities if that would help. A few weeks later, my second-line manager replied and stood by management's right to cancel the agreement but agreed to allow me to do a trial telework agreement for one day a week for the next two months. This was unacceptable because there was no resolution to the issue. Also, I viewed this as a slap in the face because of all of the sacrifices that I had made for the organization. I admit that I let my ego get in the way and instead of stepping back and letting God fight this battle, I chose to continue the fight myself. I filed a complaint against the organization alleging disability discrimination based on the Rehabilitation Act of 1973. In cases of discrimination, the government is notoriously slow to respond. The case was referred to a counselor and, after providing the person with my supporting documents, all I could do was sit and wait. In the meantime, since the telework agreement was cancelled, I was back on a Monday through Friday schedule in D.C.

Eventually, cooler heads prevailed and I was able to work out an agreement with the organization that allowed for some

Discerning God's Purpose

telework along with other flexible scheduling options that allowed me to spend more time in Austin. This was a win/win or so I initially thought. During my study time, I happened to read Romans 12:19 which says "Beloved, never avenge yourselves, but leave it to the wrath of God, for it is written, 'Vengeance is mine, I will repay,' says the Lord." When I decided to take matters into my own hands, God said, "Okay, I'll let you handle this yourself." While I may have won the battle, I was still losing the war. I was spending more time away from home, and my absence was being felt in a number of ways. Renita was feeling more and more like a single parent. Instead of raising one child, we now had three. That meant that she was arranging for home repairs to be completed, overseeing homework, dealing with school issues and more—all with little help from me. Also, she was bearing the brunt of incorporating Lezroy and Neilah into our family and the process was very painful. Not to be left out, Julia was even starting to act out because of my absence. She missed me, plus she was beginning to get a little jealous because of all of the attention paid to Lezroy and Neilah, and started to feel left out. Renita was starting to wear out. While she was maintaining our home in Texas, she was still very concerned about her mother. While I would check on her mother while I was in the D.C. area, she was still legally responsible for decisions regarding her mom's care. On top of all of that, she still had a job to do as well. All of this was too much for one person to handle.

The family was falling apart, and Julia took it upon herself to get my attention. One weekend when I was home, we were talking about her week and, in particular, something that happened at school. Before I started commuting on a regular basis, our relationship was close and she always felt comfortable talking with me about anything that came up. Now, things seemed to be different. During the time that I was on the road, the emotional distance between us began to increase. During our discussion, Julia came out and said that she really didn't feel like she knew me anymore since I was gone all of the time and didn't feel that I was there for her when she needed me. Needless to say, that hurt. At the same time, we still had a number of follow-up discussions with Penny, and she reminded me that my time on the road was most likely impacting our ability to fully incorporate Lezroy and Neilah into the family. Initially, I thought that by "only" being gone for three to four days each week, I would still have time to form a bond with them and help them to discover their purpose in life. What became apparent is that my absence was contributing to a form of abandonment that they felt was similar to what they experienced back in St. Vincent, and, therefore, they were reluctant to trust me. Since Renita would spend a lot of time helping Julia with her personal needs, Lezroy and Neilah spent a lot of time by themselves and really weren't interested in bonding as a family. We were all living under one roof, but it felt like we were still two different families.

My travel between Austin and Washington, D.C., continued for almost four years. I settled for a life of long-distance commuting to a job that I no longer enjoyed. Along with a stressful home life, the stress of long-distance travel to a job that was no longer

CHAPTER 17

fulfilling finally started to take its toll. I began experiencing health problems like back and chest pains, an increased number of cold and flu incidents and a feeling of just being tired all of the time. During my annual check-up, my doctor said that overall I was still fairly healthy, but that my recent health problems were the result of stress. Since I also reported having difficulty sleeping, my doctor referred me to an ear, nose, and throat specialist who diagnosed me with a deviated septum. I had a severe blockage in my right nostril that impacted my ability to breathe and sleep. Over time, this would get worse so he recommended surgery to fix the problem. The good news (if you could call it that) is that I would need to be home for at least two weeks to recuperate from the surgery before resuming my travel schedule.

During my time at home, I had a chance to see how my family was truly operating on a daily basis and must say that I didn't like it. Since I had a lot of time on my hands, I started thinking about our family life and the choices that I had made. I started to ask myself some pretty hard questions. Was I living to work or working to live? I wondered if I was truly fulfilling the calling that God had placed on my life or had I decided to just settle where I was? The real question that I had was what kind of legacy would I leave for my wife and my children? If I died that night, would anyone care? I was miserable, and so was my family. I knew that I was supposed to live a life of purpose, but at this point, I settled because I was afraid of change; afraid to walk away from a secure job and into the unknown, afraid of losing the material things that I had worked so hard for. The essential question was would I follow

God or continue to do things my own way? At that moment, I realized that if I didn't change, I would lose something far greater than material things. I would lose my family and ultimately my soul. I admitted that I was broken emotionally and spiritually and didn't know what to do. I got down on my knees and called on the only source who I knew could help. I told God that I knew I had made a mess of things and that my bad decisions had not only affected me but my entire family. I asked for His help in getting back on track. I committed to seeking His wisdom and guidance in all that I would do. However, as the Bible says in James 2:17, "So also faith by itself, if it does not have works, is dead." It was time to put my faith into action, but first, I needed a little push.

Discerning God's Purpose

CHAPTER 18
A SEASON OF CHANGE

When we moved to Austin, I only planned to commute for a short period of time. Eventually I knew that I would need to find work in Austin. This city is the technology epicenter of the Southwest and has one of the lowest unemployment rates in the nation, so I figured with my background, it would be fairly easy to find a job. I thought back to the lessons that I learned throughout my career when looking for employment. I remember when I just finished my master's degree in business and was looking to advance in my career. I contacted some local executive recruiting firms, retooled my resume, and within a matter of a few months, I had a new job. I figured that this would be no different. Just after we arrived in Austin, I contacted local recruiting firms, retooled my resume, but this time, things were different. I wasn't getting the responses that I was used to. Although I had been with the federal government for the past ten years, I had previous private-sector experience so I still thought that I would get some sort of feedback. This time, nothing.

I didn't have a good experience when I started my own business so I wasn't especially eager to go down that path again. I failed in operating my own business because with all of Julia's unique challenges, I chose to focus on her and not the business. We moved to Austin to accommodate Julia's educational needs so I still felt that I wouldn't be able to focus all of my efforts on starting a business. I wanted to be able to earn a living, but not at the expense of fulfilling my purpose. With the arrival of two additional children, I needed to find a way to support my growing family. Since I wasn't getting much response from local recruiting firms, I decided to look for a career or executive coach to give me some tips on ways to better compete in the local job market. I signed up for career coaching with a local firm and met with a wonderful coach named Michelle. We hit it off and bonded immediately. Instead of just updating my resume, Michelle suggested that I participate in a battery of tests, including personality profiles, to help determine what would be the right fit for this stage of my career. I had been through similar tests in the past such as the Myers-Briggs Type Indicator (MBTI) Personality test, but I decided to go into this with an open mind and followed her suggestion. I took a battery of tests, and when the results came back, it took me by surprise. While the tests showed that I was good at managing people, it also revealed that I didn't like doing it. I loved leading and mentoring people instead.

With this as a backdrop, Michelle asked me questions that made me think. From our preliminary discussions, she knew that family was very important to me. Now, she asked what else I liked to do that made me happy and fulfilled. What were the values that meant the most to me? If I could do anything for work, regardless of money, what would it be? I said that I wanted to help people,

Discerning God's Purpose

CHAPTER 18

but what exactly did I have in mind? Did I like communicating with a large number of people or was I more comfortable in a smaller setting? Considering all of the jobs that I had in the past, what did I enjoy the most and what did I like the least. On and on she went. When I started thinking about these questions and applying them to my life, I realized that I had always done what made others happy. I didn't choose a career based on the values that were important to me. Instead, my decisions were usually based on money. I chose the technology field based on how much money I could make instead of what I wanted to do. I chose to become a manager because of promotion potential instead of personal fulfillment. In short, I chose a great career but for the wrong reasons. I was successful but not fulfilled. I knew that I was a good leader because of how people looked up to me and sought my advice regardless of whether I was their supervisor or not. People thought of me as being easy to talk to and as someone who would give good advice. I was a person who could be trusted and would keep things in confidence when it came time to bare their soul. My focus was on helping them instead of promoting myself. As I continued to think, it suddenly dawned on me that I was in the wrong line of work.

My desire for a change in employment coupled with my desire to fulfill my purpose led me to look at different options, career-wise. During our coaching discussions, I shared my frustrations with my current organization. Michelle rightfully pointed out that the problem I was having wasn't the work, but the fact that the values of my job and the organization that I worked for were not in alignment with my character and values as a person. My family was extremely important to me, and it was obvious that the organization didn't support that. She also noted that my job required that I focus on managing resources and my preference for mentoring my colleagues was not something that was valued by the organization. In short, I was doing the opposite of what I wanted to do and my mind was saying enough. I needed to earn a living, but I also had a desire to help and serve others. I was happiest when I was training others to master their own purpose.

Since establishing a relationship with God in the NICU long ago, the church had become a focal point in my life. Whenever we move to a new city, one of the first things that we do is look for a church home. When we moved to Austin, we found a church that was close to where we lived. It was smaller than our previous church in Maryland; however, the teachings were biblically based and the members welcomed us with open arms. They also had a small but growing deaf ministry. We participated in various church activities, and soon I began to establish relationships with several of the men including Tom (one of the part-time assistant pastors at the church). We became fast friends because we had similar personalities, were both military veterans, and were at key crossroads in terms of our respective careers. Soon, we began meeting for brunch every few months just to talk and encourage one another. We trusted and confided in one another knowing that whatever was said stayed confidential. We agreed to meet on a particular Saturday at a local diner. Tom was running a little late so since I arrived first, I ordered our usual drinks (water and iced

Discerning God's Purpose

CHAPTER 18

tea) and looked over the menu while I waited. A few minutes later, Tom entered the restaurant and sat down across from me.

"Hey, what's going on?" I said.

"Busy," he replied. "I have to preach tonight and not only am I still trying to finish this message, but I was up late last night with a family from church." I had just got back into town the night before and hadn't heard the news about a young member of our church being killed a few nights before. "Obviously, his family is taking his death pretty hard. The police are still trying to piece together what happened. The family is planning on attending church tomorrow so I imagine that it will be a difficult service to get through" he said.

"I'm sorry to hear that," I said not knowing what else to say. "If there is anything that we can do, please let me know."

"The funeral is scheduled for Monday, and the funeral home has everything in hand. Just continue to pray for them."

After ordering our food, we spent the next few minutes catching up about each other's families as well as other idle chit-chat. Tom started to look at me intently. I started feeling a little uncomfortable so I asked, "What's wrong?"

"That is the question that I have for you" he said. "You don't seem like yourself. Is everything all right?"

"Well, not really," I replied. "I'm still trying to find a job closer to home and am not having much luck. The commute to D.C. is killing me and obviously the family isn't very happy that I am gone all of the time."

"Hmm," was all he said. After a few seconds of silence, Tom asked how things were going at work.

"OK," I said with not much enthusiasm.

"Just OK?" he asked.

"Well, I'm still fighting with my boss about me teleworking from Austin," I replied. Tom knew what was coming so he just let me vent. "I'm up in D.C. for most of the week, and when I get back home, I'm exhausted. I can do my job very well from here, but I guess they just want to see my pretty face," I said, trying to lighten the mood. I went on about how things were unfair and how other managers were still able to telework several days a week. "It's just not fair," I said.

"Well, she's the boss." Tom replied. "That's her right."

"I know, but it's just a stupid way to run a business" I said. "I mean come on. We're always talking about how to improve morale, but then management does stupid things like this."

"Well, if you don't like it, leave," Tom said. "Find something else up in D.C. until you can find something here."

After listening to me continue to drone on for a few more minutes, Tom finally got tired of my whining and cut right to the heart of the matter. "Listen Jim, I know that you aren't happy in your current job, but it's important for you to realize that it isn't your boss's job to make you happy. It's yours. If you don't like what you are doing, find something else."

Before I could interrupt, he said, "Let me finish. Your unhappiness isn't about your job; it's about your life. You made the

Discerning God's Purpose

CHAPTER 18

decision to move here, not your boss. You made the decision to commute back and forth to D.C., not your boss. You made all of the decisions, so why are you blaming your boss because you are unhappy?"

Before I could give an answer, Tom cut me off. "You talk about travel, teleworking, and all of that but that isn't the real reason for your unhappiness. The real reason is that you are not doing what God intended for you to do. You want to do things on your own but are ignoring what God is trying to tell you. Until that changes, nothing else will matter. You will never be happy there. Let me ask you another question, why are you still there?"

"Simple, it pays the bills," I replied. "Well," Tom replied, "if the only reason that you are there is for the money, then you have essentially become a prostitute."

"Hey," I protested, but again Tom cut me off.

"I'm sorry if that offends you, but it's true. You have to remember that your job is not the source of your money, God is. You talk about having faith but aren't showing it. The real reason that you aren't happy is because you aren't fulfilling your purpose, and God is letting you know it. He is asking you to trust Him, but until you do, nothing is going to change." For a moment, I was speechless. I had never had anyone talk to me like this in my life. Tom's face softened and he continued, "Jim, I love you like a little brother. I'm not trying to hurt you but am only trying to help. Right now, you are thinking that your boss is the reason for your unhappiness, but it isn't. It seems to me that God is trying to close a door but you keep standing in the way. It's time for you to enter into a new season."

After a few minutes of silence, I finally looked at Tom and said, "What should I do next?"

"Simple—shut up and listen," Tom said with a sly smile. "He'll tell you what to do if you are quiet. All you have to do is listen. Remember God's word. 'I know the plans I have for you,' declares the Lord, 'plans for welfare and not for evil, to give you a future and a hope.' ... Remember, God's got your back. All you have to do is to trust Him." Then he looked at his watch, motioned to our waitress and said, "It's late and I have to go. I have to finish my message for tonight's service. See you at church tomorrow."

"OK," I said.

As he got up, he said, "Remember, shut up and listen. Love you little brother," and then turned to leave. As I watched his back, I sat there wondering what I would do next.

On the way home, I started thinking about what Tom said. As much as I didn't want to admit it, Tom was right. My unhappiness was about more than just the commute. It was about control. I wanted the American dream, but I wanted to do it my way. I had a good job and was reluctant to give it up. My family and I had a comfortable lifestyle, and I didn't want to do anything to mess that up. I guess it went back to lessons that I was taught as a child. My parents always said, "Go get your education; get a good job, work hard and then you will be successful." I followed this advice, and up to this point had what most would consider a successful career.

Discerning God's Purpose

CHAPTER 18

Now, when I should be enjoying the fruits of my labor, God was asking me to do something else. He was asking me to give up control and to follow a new path. Just like before, He was putting me to the test. As I was driving home from my meeting with Tom, I realized that the pregnancy and the ensuing tragedy was a major turning point in my life. I knew that my purpose was to prepare Julia, Lezroy, and Neilah for whatever assignment God had for them. I also knew that by being on the road every week, I wasn't fulfilling my purpose. As I grew in my relationship with God, I began to turn to Him whenever I had a major decision to make. I wanted to do what was in the best interest of my family but I also didn't want to put us into a financial bind. I began to pray for guidance on what to do.

Over the years, I have learned that God always answers prayers; however, it may not be in the way that I would want. There is an old saying that God may not come when you want Him, but He will always be right on time. My parents and my mother-in-law still lived in the D.C. area, and I used my weekly commutes to also check on them. Shortly after moving to Austin, my parents decided to sell their home of more than thirty years and move into a senior community where help would be available in looking after their needs. I was able to rest easy knowing that someone was looking out for them when I was not there. Unfortunately, the news wasn't as good for my mother-in-law. With Renita working full time in Texas and taking the primary role in caring for our children, I took her place in caring for her mom. I checked in on her weekly and was able to be with her during numerous stays in the hospital. Eventually, the complications associated with Alzheimer's disease became too much for her, and she finally went home to be with the Lord. We were able to care for her when she needed us most and now she was resting in our Savior's arms. Although we still miss her very much, I sensed that God was arranging things for me to return to fulfilling my purpose. It was time for me to come home.

Making such a major change would not only involve me but my family as well. My family is critically important to me, and before making this transition, I needed their support. For me, that means having my parents' support as well as my immediate family. Growing up, my parents raised me to be independent and to only rely on others when absolutely necessary. I must say that there have only been a few times in my life when I have needed to "come home" and ask for help. For the most part, though, I have been self-sufficient. After the move to Texas, my parents helped us lower our expenses by offering a place to stay during our commutes back "home" for work. Although they were self-sufficient living in the senior community, I was still their only son and needed to be available if and when needed. That being said, they still encouraged me to find a job in my same career field so that I could maintain my current standard of living. When it became evident that a change in my vocation was coming, my parents became concerned. I even remember my Dad saying, "You can't just quit. You have to provide for your family." However, as he saw the toll that the commute and not living my purpose was taking on my health and overall wellbeing, he began to have a change of

CHAPTER 18

heart. Finally, he simply said, "You know what you are doing. Do what you think is best."

I'll never forget a conversation that I had with my mom shortly before I decided to resign. Sometimes, I would share with her what was going on at work, with my health, and some of the issues that we were having as a family. As only a mother could do, she simply said, "It's time for you to go home and be with your family. Dad and I are fine and are still doing pretty well. I know that you will be there when we need you, but right now, you need to go home. The kids need you. Renita needs you. Besides, you won't do them any good if you continue to ignore your health and wind up dead. Things will work out, but you need to go home."

She also told me of how something similar happened to my Dad right before he decided to retire. Things had gotten very stressful for him at work, and Mom was worried that one day he would have a heart attack because of the stress. Since I had finished college and was now out on my own, they were able to adjust their lifestyle to accommodate him leaving the workforce. I remember after Dad retired, my mom also decided to accept a buyout from her company and come home to begin a new life. Neither of my parents are the type to just sit around. My mom decided to work on a variety of short-term government commissions and my Dad decided to go sell real estate. My mom reminded me that they were able to successfully transition to a new phase in life when they were around my age, and she had no doubt that I would be able to do the same. They also reminded me that we were family.

"If you need anything, just let us know." My parents were on board. Now it was time to talk to my wife and kids.

Renita and I have been married for over twenty-six years. When we were dating, I told her of my dreams to one day own my own business. We were both young and in love, so of course she expressed support for me to follow my dream. After we got married, established our household and expanded our family, she became a little bit more hesitant in supporting my dream. Right after Julia was born, we went through a rocky period that threatened us financially. By now, we had dug ourselves out of our financial hole and were finally beginning to enjoy the fruits of our labor when this season of change came upon us. She had been fine with moving to Austin since the plan was for both of us to maintain our employment. Now, I was talking about leaving my safe and secure job to step out into the unknown.

Dave Ramsey is a radio personality, speaker, and the author of several financial books and courses including the best-seller titled *Financial Peace*. Dave started out investing in real estate and experienced some early successes; however, changes in the tax laws during the late 1980s caused him to lose everything and forced him to file for bankruptcy. In order to not repeat his mistakes, he became an expert on what the Bible teaches about money and also read everything that he could get his hands on regarding proper money management. I attended one of his courses called Financial Peace. In the course, one of the things that he talks about is the role of money in a marriage. He speaks about the fact that women have something called a "security gland," where they

Discerning God's Purpose

must feel safe and secure at all times, especially when it comes to money. He states that men must learn to address this concern if they are to have a successful marriage. My wife is the personification of this statement.

When I first started thinking of leaving my job, Renita thought that I was nuts. She would say that we had a house and three kids. What was I going to do? How were we going to maintain our standard of living? On and on, the questions kept coming. At the same time, she could see the effect that the travel and the stress was having on my health. She knew that I was doing everything that I could to find another job but that God was calling me to do something else. Besides, she was also feeling the effects of her own stress of having to spend most her time as a "single" mom and desperately needed my help. Lastly, she could see the effect that my absence was having on the kids, especially Julia. She knew that I needed to be home, but she was still scared. I knew that her security was threatened, and I wanted to alleviate her anxiety as much as possible. Ever since we were introduced to Dave Ramsey and Financial Peace, we have kept a budget. We weren't debt free, but over the years, we were able to reduce our debt load quite a bit. One Saturday morning, I reviewed our budget with her and showed how we could survive for a period of time on one income. It wouldn't be pretty, and we would forgo a lot of luxuries but it was doable. We both knew that I wouldn't sit at home forever, but she also had the security of knowing that we were in no danger of losing our home. She still wasn't comfortable with only one income, but she knew that this was a step that I needed to take. She told me that she supported my decision to make a change. Now, to tell the kids.

Before moving to Texas, Julia saw me every day. I rarely traveled for work but when I did, I was only gone for a day or two. Now, she only saw me on weekends. When Lezroy and Neilah joined the family, I was already on the road, and so that is what they were used to. Julia would frequently tell me that she wanted me home more but had gradually become accustomed to this new lifestyle. After Renita and I decided that I would come home, we decided to take the kids out to dinner to tell them the news. Julia was predictably very excited, but Lezroy and Neilah were a little more subdued. They were used to me not being there for the majority of the time, and sometimes with young children, change can be difficult. During the week, things were a little less structured as Renita did her best to keep up with all three kids. With me being around more, I told them that there would be more structure but that we would have more time for them. Lezroy was concerned with how I was going to make money and how we would survive. He and Neilah had been through some tough times before the adoption, and obviously didn't want to go through that again. We explained to them that while we may reduce our standard of living, we would be just fine. Julia didn't care how, she was just happy that I would be home. Lezroy and Neilah just shrugged their shoulders and followed their big sister's lead. If Julia was fine then so were they. Now, that the family was on board, it was time to see what I would do next. It was time to pull over in the car of life and let God to take the wheel.

Discerning God's Purpose

CHAPTER 19
HAVING FAITH

Outside of the two years that I owned my own business, I always worked for someone else. Since I was thirteen years old, I never had a problem finding a job. When we moved to Austin, I looked for a job in my career field and found nothing. I tried everything that I could to stay in that nice, safe, and secure environment, but after four years of looking, it was clear that God was nudging me in a new direction. I would have to give up that sense of security and go out on my own. I must admit that I was scared, but when I asked for help, God showed up in an unusual way. At first, I started small and asked Him to provide me with a job. He replied by saying that He would "supply all of my needs according to His riches" (Philippians 4:19). Great, I thought, then help me win the lottery (that was my idea of a bold prayer). He replied by pointing me to scripture that says, "Wealth gained hastily will dwindle, but whoever gathers little by little will increase it" (Proverbs 13). With no job in sight, I started to get angry and asked God if He had led me to Austin only to leave me in my own personal "desert." God didn't get mad but reminded me of His instruction to read the Bible. At that moment, I remembered something that my friend Pastor Tom once told me. During one of our brunch meetings, Tom told me of how he reads a verse or two of Proverbs every morning before starting his day. I remember him telling me that by reading Proverbs, he was actually praying for wisdom on a daily basis. He said that by reading Proverbs, he was able to call on the Lord to help him make decisions in his daily life. In doing so, he was constantly reminded of the path that God had for him. I smiled as I thought back to Tom's advice to "shut up and listen." Well, I guess this was God's way of confirming what Tom said. If it was good enough for Tom, then it was good enough for me.

I can't say that I read the Bible on a daily basis, but I can say that I do read the Book of Proverbs often in order to gain the wisdom that I need for everyday life. When I started to accept God's wisdom, I started asking God to reveal His plan for this stage of my life. He started by showing me Proverbs 2:3-5 which says, "if you call out for insight and raise your voice for understanding, if you seek it like silver and search for it as for hidden treasures, then you will understand the fear of the LORD and find the knowledge of God." I gained a deeper understanding of the value of integrity when I read "For the upright will inhabit the land, and those with integrity will remain in it, but the wicked will be cut off from the land, and the treacherous will be rooted out of it" (Proverbs 2:21-22). I began to reflect on my own experiences of when I did the right things for the right reasons, my efforts were generally successful. I would read Proverbs and compare His teachings to my experiences in life and realized that God truly did have me in the palm of His hand and when I followed His plan, I was successful. I remembered when I found myself at life's crossroads and didn't

Discerning God's Purpose

CHAPTER 19

know what to do (like when I decided to leave the Army and come home with no job and a new wife), God was always with me. I smiled as I read Proverbs 3:5-6 where it says "trust in the Lord with all your heart and lean not unto your own understanding" and "when you acknowledge Him, He will make straight your paths." When I left the Army, I had a place to return to and very soon thereafter, a job that allowed me to pay my bills. God also showed that I had a wife who took our marriage vows seriously and stuck by my side whether I was "rich or poor; or whether in "sickness or in good health." By reading Proverbs, I started to see similarities in other scriptures such as Deuteronomy 31:6 which says "It is the LORD who goes before you. He will be with you; he will not leave you or forsake you. Do not fear or be dismayed." As I continued to read, my confidence in and understanding of God's word began to grow. I knew that by following His lead, the Lord would always be with me. I just needed to have faith.

While I knew that God would be with me, I wasn't stupid enough to think that everything would be easy. I remember my father's words when I was growing up. He said, "If you want something you have to work for it." My dad is not a person who sits and reads the Bible on a daily basis, but his words of wisdom were similar in many ways. When Dad told me the story of Air Force General B.O. Davis, Jr. and how he made it his personal goal to graduate from the U.S. Military Academy despite being shunned by his classmates because of his skin color, he was actually teaching me the lesson that I later learned in Proverbs 6:4-5 which says, "Give your eyes no sleep and your eyelids no slumber; save yourself like a gazelle from the hand of the hunter, like a bird from the hand of the fowler."

In addition to my father, I met others who served as positive influences as well. I had a friend in college who had a desire to open a business of his own. He would always quote Proverbs 6:6-11 which says, "Go to the ant, O sluggard; consider her ways, and be wise. Without having any chief, officer, or ruler, she prepares her bread in summer and gathers her food in harvest. How long will you lie there, O sluggard? When will you arise from your sleep? A little sleep, a little slumber, a little folding of the hands to rest, and poverty will come upon you like a robber, and want like an armed man." He would also quote President Franklin Roosevelt and say that "the only thing that we have to fear is fear itself." When I was in college, I hated statistics. It always gave me fits. One day, after walking out of a particular class in disgust, I remember a professor passing me in the hall. He stopped me and quoted Jesus in Matthew 17:20 by saying "if you have faith like a grain of mustard seed, you will say to this mountain, 'Move from here to there,' and it will move, and nothing will be impossible for you." I ended up passing the class.

As I began to remember these instances, my thoughts soon changed from focusing on fear to expecting success. I also began to draw inspiration from the most unlikely of places. I saw my youngest two children Lezroy and Neilah, whom we had just adopted less than a year before, leave everything and everyone that they knew, relocate to a new country, learn two new languages (English and American Sign Language), and start to do well. I

Discerning God's Purpose

CHAPTER 19

saw my oldest daughter Julia, the one who doctors said would never walk and would barely be able to read above a fourth-grade level, consistently make the honor roll in a regular academic environment but also face her fears and make the high school cheerleading team. I began to think nothing is impossible, as long as you try and give your very best. As Jesus said in Matthew 19:26, "With men this is impossible, but with God everything is possible." I knew that I could be successful, but I couldn't do it alone. I am lucky to be married to a Proverbs 31 woman who is "far more precious than jewels." She truly has my complete trust and I know that "she does me good, and not harm, all the days of her life." I have others who I can turn to for help for as Proverbs 15:22 says, "Without counsel plans fail, but with many advisers they succeed."

I knew that whatever was in store as the next step in life, my children would be watching. Since my job was to prepare all three for whatever God had in store for them, the first thing that I needed to do was to teach them the ways of Christ. The best thing that I could give them was wisdom. I knew that by learning and living the examples taught in Proverbs, I would be able to pass that wisdom onto my children. I knew that my ultimate measure of success would not come from my career achievements or how much money I made, it would come from how I prepared my children for this journey called life. Many people measure their worth with money but as a wise man once told me right after Julia was born, "if you fail as a father, you aren't worth much."

CHAPTER 20
A NEW CHAPTER

When I made the decision to leave my job in D.C., I was uncertain as to what would come next. I didn't know what I was going to do next. All I had to depend on was my faith that God would provide. I remember praying "OK Lord, if this is what you want me to do then I can't do this alone. I need your help." Shortly after making the decision to leave, I found out that my organization would soon be offering buyouts to any employee who wanted to resign from the government. I took this as a sign from God and decided to apply. I thought that if it was meant to be, I would be approved for the buyout. The buyout was generous enough where we would be able to maintain our standard of living as a family until I figured out what to do next. It took about a month, but sure enough, my buyout request was approved. Now, my decision to leave was final. I was showing God that my faith in Him was total.

I left my position with a fairly substantial financial cushion, but I knew that it wouldn't last forever. I needed to find another career but I also knew that my new career needed to line up with my purpose. After moving to Austin, working with a career coach and now being open to finding a new line of work, I began to look at the different opportunities that were available in my new

CHAPTER 20

hometown. Although God closed the chapter on my real estate career twelve years prior, I still had a sense that real estate was in my future. I just didn't know how. I did decide to be open to whatever opportunities God decided to bring across my path. As I looked around at employment options in Austin, one company that I constantly ran across was Keller Williams Realty. Keller Williams (KW) was the largest real estate franchise in North America and had the largest market presence in Austin. According to the Austin Chamber of Commerce and the local business journal, KW was one of the best companies to work for in Austin. I knew about one of the founders of KW, Gary Keller, because some of the books that he has written. His bestselling books *The Millionaire Real Estate Agent* and *The Millionaire Real Estate Investor* are classic, how-to book on succeeding in real estate. He followed those books with the wildly successful business book *The ONE Thing: The Surprisingly Simple Truth Behind Extraordinary Results*. I found the book to really be an extension of the company mission statement: To build careers worth having, businesses worth owning, and lives worth living.

KW was founded in 1983 by Gary Keller and Joe Williams. From the start, Gary made it a point to design the company around the needs of its agents, not the other way around. KW has established a reputation as a high-performing organization by concentrating on three things:

- A Life by Design: Most of KW's workforce consists of Realtors who are also independent contractors. As with most contractors, Realtors like to work in an environment where they are happiest and are most fulfilled. With this in mind, KW asks each new agent or employee to think about the life that they would like to lead and then to design a business around that. The goal is to have people think about and have success in all phases of their lives, not just one part.

- Winning with Integrity: KW is also a market leader that only wants to succeed based on its core set of beliefs. These beliefs guide how it conducts business as well as how it treats their workforce. KW relies on these beliefs to create the systems, products, and services that lead to productivity and profitability.

- Putting its workforce first: KW believes in putting people in a position to succeed by constantly training its workforce. Most people think of KW as a Real Estate Brokerage. What isn't as widely known is that KW is also the number-one training organization in the world according to *Training Magazine*. In his book *The ONE Thing*, Gary asks an essential question: What's the ONE Thing you can do such that by doing it everything else will be easier or unnecessary? KW's training component, KW MAPS Coaching, is designed to help its workforce answer that question and then to offer tools to maximize their probability of success. The main goal of KW MAPS coaching is to offer "programs for real estate professionals and business leaders to transform their businesses and lives through education and coaching." It offers many different programs for agents and employees to define develop and refine success on their own terms.

Discerning God's Purpose

CHAPTER 20

These three principles were appealing to me because it would allow me to focus on my purpose of raising my children to be ready for whatever God has in store while also pursuing my calling to help others. I liked the leadership philosophy that allowed me to design a career that was best for me. Lastly, Keller Williams priorities of placing your relationship with God first, your family second, and then your work no higher than third was the same philosophy that I believed in. This was a company whose values were closely aligned with mine. I also looked at Keller Williams (KW) not only because of the status as a leading employer in the Austin real estate industry but also because of its reputation for integrity.

I decided to meet with Diane, one of the co-team leaders for the local Keller Williams Office in Austin, to see if KW would be a good fit. What immediately impressed me about her was that she initially asked me about my life, my goals, and my expectations before saying anything about what KW had to offer. Once she had an idea of where I was headed, she explained the KW model and how I could use it to get where I wanted to go. She focused on me being able to define a career path that best suited me instead of what was best for KW. With a heavy focus on training and development, I could see how KW helps its workforce its succeed in whatever part of the business the agent chooses. I also learned about KW's philanthropic arm, KW Cares. I learned how KW helps local offices connect with the communities that it serves through various charitable events. That was something that was very important to me. After learning about all that KW had to offer, I could think of no place else that I would rather be.

After becoming licensed and officially joining KW, the first thing all new agents are required to complete is the new agent training program called *Ignite*. This program introduces new agents to the policies as well as the tools necessary to get started. Since I had been away from the real estate game for a while, Diane also connected me with Julie, the director of career development for our office, for some one-on-one coaching. Julie was a successful agent for over fifteen years before pursuing her passion for training new agents. Julie met with me to help establish my initial goals. Since I didn't have an extensive marketing background, she encouraged me to try techniques such as door knocking, open houses, and social media campaigns to determine what worked best for me. I can remember her main point to try out a bunch of things at first but then pick something and be consistent. During these coaching and subsequent training sessions, it became very clear that I was not suited to be your "normal" real estate agent. I didn't enjoy doing the typical "sales" activities but I still liked the values of the company and wanted to be a part of it. I also liked the fact that KW didn't offer you a "job" but an opportunity to determine your own path. I knew I wanted to stay with KW, but I didn't quite know what that role would be.

Sometimes, the inspiration for change will come from unexpected places. In my last job, I worked within an organization where English was a second language for the majority of the

CHAPTER 20

workforce. One day at work, my boss asked me to write a report for her to submit to senior management who in turn would submit a summarized version to Congress. I didn't want to do it, but I still took on the assignment and gave it my best. I finished the report, submitted it to my boss, and then went back to other things. The report was so well received that my boss began asking me to write additional things on her behalf. I received so many requests that soon I began to feel like her speechwriter instead of the chief of staff. At first, I complained about the writing assignments but then I started to look forward to them. I started to remember the joy that I had in writing as a child. I still didn't like the work environment but this was one aspect of my job that I did enjoy. A few days later, I read an article on Tyler Perry in which he shared advice that he received from Oprah Winfrey to write down your thoughts as a way of providing a form of psychological relief from stressful situations. I decided to give it a try.

During one of my brunch meetings with Tom, I decided to tell him about my new hobby. Since many of my colleagues regularly sought my advice and counsel, I told him that I started writing a journal containing tips on leadership and management. Not only was Tom excited for me, but he encouraged me to go further and share my tips with a wider audience. In addition to Tom, I also shared my work with other close confidants who encouraged me as well. Many told me outright that they thought I had found my true calling. I could see how writing would be fulfilling to me and would help me in fulfilling my purpose. The biggest question that

I had was how to turn my new hobby into a business. For that, I went to see three people whom I had come to respect who now have become valuable business mentors to me.

I met Ken at a company barbecue a few months after joining Keller Williams. Ken is a successful agent who regularly gives of his time to help those of us who are just getting started. What I really liked about Ken is that he recognized that there was no one way to build a business and that each individual should focus on what is right for them. Not too long ago, Julie decided to move to another role with KW, and Ken was one of the people selected to replace her. A few months after his selection, Ken reached out to tell me that even though I wasn't a new agent, he was still happy to help me in building my business. Since I was still figuring out what I wanted to do, I figured that meeting with him would be a good idea. When we met, I was honest and said that I really wasn't interested in selling real estate in a traditional sense but that I still liked KW and the values that it stood for and wanted to create a business that was right for me. I told him about my new hobby (writing) and that I wanted to see how I could incorporate that into whatever I decided to do next. I recently attended an information session about profit sharing and how some agents use that as the basis of their business. Ken thought that this would be a wonderful opportunity for me and could see how I could use my writing as a way to attract talent. Since I liked the values of KW and also liked to write, I could use my platform to share my experiences and become a recruiter for KW. This seemed like a great

CHAPTER 20

fit because it allowed me to fulfill my purpose and focus my business on an area that I loved. He also reminded me that KW had a great profit-sharing incentive for bringing in new agents and that I could potentially earn more over the long run doing that than simply by selling real estate. I remember leaving the office that day feeling like I was floating on air.

Next, I met with Diane and her partner Melanie, the other co-team leader for the office, to talk about how I could successfully transition into this part of the business. By now, I had started writing about KW in my own blog and as a contributor on other well-known leadership platforms. Not only did they think it was a wonderful idea, but they were willing to share their own leadership philosophy as a way to help me get started. From that meeting, I came away with ideas on ways that I could share KW's leadership philosophy as well as key reasons for KW's success. In short, I really did find my calling and ironically it was right in front of me the whole time. I recently read an interview that DJ Khaled and Tony Robbins did for the cover story of *Complex Magazine*. These two leaders come from very different backgrounds and are successful in completely different industries; however, many of their keys to success are the same. One thing they both said that the key to their success was learning to not chase after money but to focus on serving people. "If you serve people better than anyone else, you won't have to chase after money, the money will chase after you." I remember thinking that that is one of the main reasons for KW's success and how I wanted that to be the basis for my new life. Instead of asking what I will get, I now focus on asking what I can give. I realized that if I approach life with that mindset, I would never have anything to worry about. From that point forward, I began to enjoy the journey.

Discerning God's Purpose

CONCLUSION
COMING FULL CIRCLE

On that sunny day in June, we arrived at Good Sam to visit the place where it all started. We called a few days ahead of time to let them know that one of their "graduates" would be returning for a visit. We went up to the NICU and met one of the social workers who arranged for us to tour the new and improved NICU. Lezroy and Neilah decided to go to the waiting room while Julia, Renita, and I went in for the tour. It was like stepping back in time. The sights, sounds, and smells brought back instant memories. Julia was a little sad at first because this was, after all, the place where two of her siblings died. We went over to the same area where Julia spent the first few months of life and just reminisced about how far she had come. We saw some of the same nurses who were on duty when Julia was there and had a number of very happy reunions. By now, Julia had started to come around and began to feel like her old self. She even allowed me to take a picture of her in the same type of chair that I used for skin to skin "kangaroo care" with her as an infant that studies show have lifesaving benefits for preemies. Julia saw the very small diapers that she used as a newborn and saw firsthand all of the love and care that these nurses provide that was the key to her survival.

CONCLUSION

Many of the nurses who cared for Julia when she was a baby said that they weren't surprised at Julia's progress because even then, they could see that she was a fighter. They also complimented us on how we raised Julia to be a confident young woman. I remember toward the end of the tour, we saw a young woman who was about to exit the NICU. She was obviously still a patient in the hospital and looked like she had just given birth to a baby who was now in the NICU. She was being pushed in a wheelchair (I guess to go back to her room) and was crying. I let her pass me but something told me to turn around and talk to her. I said "Excuse me, Miss. I know that this is a very tough environment and you are worried about your baby." I then pointed to Julia and said "She was born at twenty-four weeks and six days and weighed one pound six ounces. She is now sixteen and is in a regular school program, is on the honor roll, and is getting ready for college. She made it so there is every reason that your baby can make it too." I told her that there was no better place for her baby than where she was. She looked at Julia and said, "really?" I said yes. I told her that medicine had improved greatly since Julia was there and that she should have faith that her baby not only would survive but would thrive. She thanked me for sharing my story and left. Looking back, I know that God placed us there at that particular point in time so that we could give hope to that young woman. We were blessed to be a blessing.

Not too long after returning home from our trip, I made one last flight to D.C. as a government employee. I took a few months leave before returning for one final time. On my last day, I stopped by to see several colleagues one more time to just say goodbye. One of my last stops was to see a colleague whom I will call Anna. Anna was a fairly new manager, having been in her position for about a year and a half. She was great in the technical aspects of her position but needed more time and training to develop into a seasoned management professional. Although she was eager to learn, Anna hadn't had the opportunity to take any management training courses since starting in her management position. I had mentored Anna on some of the basics of management so I was especially sad to have to tell her goodbye. After the usual chit-chat and wishes of good luck, Anna asked if I had any final words of advice. I recommended a course for her to take on leadership whenever she got the opportunity and suggested a few outside organizations for her to join for professional development. As I got up to leave, she asked how I learned to be such a good manager. I said, "Simple, I became a parent."

She said, "I'm a parent too but I sure didn't learn any of this in raising my children. What's your secret?"

I said "My secret is that I never think as a manager but as a leader."

"What's the difference?" she asked.

"A manager manages resources, a leader leads people," I replied. Then I grabbed a piece of paper, wrote ten sentences down, and then handed the paper to her. "Here" I said. "These are ten leadership tips that have been the key to my success."

Discerning God's Purpose

CONCLUSION

Leaders must be led

Have High **E**xpectations

Be **A**ccountable for your own actions

Don't settle for anything less than God's best

Embrace change

Remember to serve others first

Seek Wisdom

Have Courage

Integrity comes first

Be **P**assionate about your path

"That's it?" she said.

"That's it," I replied. "There are many things that you need to be an effective manager, but these ten things are key to good leadership. Spend some time learning these things and I guarantee you will be a great leader."

With that, I returned to my office, packed up my remaining personal belongings and closed the door and the chapter on this part of my life. Walking out, I wasn't sad about closing a chapter; I was excited about what would come next. I don't know what God has in store, but as it says in Ephesians 3:20, "God is able to do far more abundantly than all that we ask or think, according to the power at work within us." I can't wait to see what tomorrow brings.

APPENDIX

ACKNOWLEDGEMENTS

Wow, I never thought that I would write a book. I just didn't think that I had an interesting story to tell. I always did what I thought was right, and I expected everyone else to do the same. I started thinking of writing a book toward the end of my tenure with the government. I was encouraged by so many colleagues to write a book about leadership, but I didn't want to come across as a big know-it-all. If I were going to write a book, I wanted to be open, honest, and transparent. I wanted to talk about my successes and my failures so that you the reader could learn from my mistakes. I am not perfect by any means. I made mistakes and lots of them (just ask my wife). The key was trying not to make the same mistake twice.

There are so many who are responsible for helping me with this book. I can't hope to name everyone who has helped me along the way but there are a chosen few who I would like to call out. First and foremost, I must thank my Lord and Savior, Jesus Christ. In the Book of Matthew (19:26), Jesus says: "With man, this is impossible but with God all things are possible."

ACKNOWLEDGEMENTS

Before anyone else, I want to thank my wife Renita for her love and support not only for this project but throughout our twenty-six years of marriage. I love you more today than the day that I met you. You are truly my virtuous wife, and my faith and trust in you is total. You have been a great partner to me and a wonderful mother for our children. I thank God every day that you are by my side.

To my children, Julia, Lezroy, and Neilah. You are my purpose. I love you more than I can tell. I thank God every day that I am your dad. I know that life has not always been easy, but I am very proud of the young ladies and gentleman that you have become.

To my parents, James and Margretta Kennedy. Simply saying "Thank You" just doesn't seem to be enough to express all of the love and appreciation that I have for you. All that I teach my children, I have learned from you. Through your actions, you showed what leadership is all about. Thank you for your tough love when I was growing up. I may not have appreciated it at the time, but without a doubt, you are responsible for the man I am today.

To Horace and Ella Richardson. Even though you are no longer with us, I want to thank you for raising Renita to be such a strong and confident woman. You are sorely missed.

To all of the branches of my family. Blessed are the ties that bind. Whether near or multiple generations removed, thank you for your love and support. You are cherished.

ACKNOWLEDGEMENTS

To my editor, Erica Orloff. You have truly been a Godsend. This may be my story, but I believe that this is our book. Your suggestions made it sing. Thank you from the bottom of my heart.

To Pastor Freddie T. Piphus of Zion Global Ministries. I want to thank you for leading me into a deeper relationship with the Lord. I'll never forget how you were there for me during my time of need when RJ, Jamie, and Julia were born. You were more than my pastor, you were my friend.

To Pastor Scott C. Moore and the members of Judah Temple A.M.E. Zion Church. You took Julia by the hand and through the deaf ministry sparked a desire to learn more about God. You baptized her in the Holy Spirit and started her journey to Christ. For that, Renita and I will forever be grateful.

To Pastor John Jenkins and the members of First Baptist Church of Glenarden. You showed that with God, anything is possible. You showed us what it is like to be spirit-led. On a personal note, you baptized me and encouraged my renewed faith in Jesus Christ. For that, I will be eternally grateful.

To Pastor Rex Johnson and the members of Christian Life Church in Austin, Texas. You welcomed this East Coast city slicker and his family into your congregation with open arms. You not only talked about your faith but showed it on a daily basis. I learned so much from you. Through the word, you showed me to Have Faith and reminded me that if God be for me, who can be against me.

Discerning God's Purpose

ACKNOWLEDGEMENTS

You also introduced me to two men who became men of faith and spiritual brothers in my time of transition—

To Vernon Cooper, Tom Travizza, and Gary Fink–my brothers in Christ. The three of you have poured more into me than you will ever know. You are good examples of what it means to be Holy Rollers (Men of God).

To Pastor Randy Phillips and the members of Life Austin Church. I owe so much to you, my church family. You encouraged me to put action behind my faith. You showed how God can take a little and by faith turn it into much. You put us on your back and carried us for a wild ride with a lot of "A-ha" moments along the way. You, along with Pastor RT, Pastor Julie and Pastor David, encouraged me to follow the path that God has for me and that if I follow His Path, He will always make a way.

I would like to thank Diane, Melanie, Julie, Ken and all the folks at the Keller Williams Market Center number one in Austin, Texas. Even though I was unsure of my path, you gave me the time, space and support to help me find my way. It wasn't easy but you never wavered in your support. For that, I am extremely grateful.

To Gary Keller, Mo Anderson, and the leadership of Keller Williams. Thank you for creating a company where lives are truly transformed. The values of God first, family second and business third is what originally attracted me to the company and is the main reason why I am still here today. You led the way in building

ACKNOWLEDGEMENTS

a brand based on integrity, service and trust. Keller Williams is truly a place where teamwork makes the dream work and I am honored to be a part of the KW family.

To the many friends and business associates whom I didn't mention but have impacted my journey in some way, thank you from the bottom of my heart.

Last but not least, I want to thank two people whom I have never met. Tyler Perry and Oprah Winfrey. Many times, Tyler Perry shared a story of how he was inspired to write by watching an episode of the Oprah Winfrey Show. She said that writing a journal was cathartic and would provide psychological help in getting through occasional rough patches in this journey we call life. I know that you have millions of fans who say that your words changed their life, but this book is living proof that you changed mine. By journaling my thoughts, I was able to see that not only did I have a story to tell but I am able to contribute leadership lessons that can help those who follow. I may not be able to thank you in person, but I can do the next best thing and that is to pass it forward.

Discerning God's Purpose

SMALL GROUP STUDY GUIDE

According to the Merriam-Webster dictionary, leadership is defined as the power or ability to lead other people. Businessdictionary.com states that leadership involves:

- Establishing a clear vision,
- Sharing that vision with others so that they will follow willingly,
- Providing the information, knowledge, and methods to realize that vision, and
- Coordinating and balancing the conflicting interests of all members and stakeholders.

Those are accurate definitions of leadership; however, I like to follow what the Bible says about Christian leadership. In 1 Timothy 3:2-5, the Bible says: "An overseer must be above reproach, the husband of one wife, sober-minded, self-controlled, respectable, hospitable, able to teach, not a drunkard, not violent but gentle, not quarrelsome, not a lover of money. He must manage his own household well, with all dignity keeping his children submissive, for if someone does not know how to manage his own household, how will he care for God's church?"

As Christians, our primary purpose is to follow the teachings of Jesus by making "Disciples of all nations, baptizing them in the name of the Father and of the Son and of the Holy Spirit, teaching them to observe all that I have commanded you" (Matthew 28:19-20). The Bible refers to this passage as "The Great Commission." As believers, we have all been given unique gifts to accomplish this purpose; however, whatever we do, "whether you eat or drink, or whatever you do, do all to the glory of God" (1 Corinthians 10:31).

Our job is to find and develop our gifts so that we may glorify God. This book showcases my journey as I discovered my unique gifts that helped me to clarify my purpose. Now, I would like to lead you on a journey to discover your own. Over the next few pages, I describe the lessons that were critical to my journey. I will also share a scripture reference and pose a few questions that will help give you Clarity of Purpose. My prayer is that this study guide will help lead you to become the person that God created you to be.

LESSON: LEADERS MUST BE LED

Chapter 5: Establish a Relationship with God

Scripture Verse: For I know the plans I have for you, declares the Lord, plans for welfare[a] and not for evil, to give you a future and a hope. (Jeremiah 29:11).

Summary: In this chapter, I discover a new level of faith and establish a relationship with God. I discuss how my relationship with God starts out with anger (mine), how I expressed my true feelings about what happened to RJ and Jamie, and finally, in my brokenness, I admitted that I didn't know what to do for Julia. It is in this chapter where I first asked God for help and discover God's true love for me.

Scenario: Think of a time when you went through a difficult or painful situation. It could be a death of a loved one, a painful divorce, or a business failure.

Questions:
1. Did you try to fix it yourself or ask for help?

LESSON: LEADERS MUST BE LED

2. If you called on God, were you filled with anxiety or did you have a sense of peace?

3. Did you still struggle with the situation, or did you suddenly see a way out?

LESSON: EXPECT THE BEST

Chapter 6: Going Home

Scripture Verse: Fear not, for I am with you; be not dismayed, for I am your God; I will strengthen you, I will help you, I will uphold you with my righteous right hand" (Isaiah 41:10).

Summary: In this chapter, Renita and I take Julia home from the hospital and were filled with fear and trepidation. We felt that we were on our own and had no one to turn to. Ultimately, we did have a number of unexpected tests but in the end, things turned out just fine.

Scenario: Think of a time when you were afraid to do something.

Questions:
1. Did you think of all the things that could go wrong, or did you think of the good things that could happen if you moved forward?

2. Did you let fear stop you, or did you have the courage to move forward?

LESSON: EXPECT THE BEST

3. Why did you make the decision that you did?

4. If you faced the same decision again, would you make the same decision?

LESSON: BE ACCOUNTABLE FOR YOUR OWN ACTIONS

Chapter 17: A Season of Change

Scripture Verse: Brothers, if anyone is caught in any transgression, you who are spiritual should restore him in a spirit of gentleness. Keep watch on yourself, lest you too be tempted. Bear one another's burdens, and so fulfill the law of Christ. For if anyone thinks he is something, when he is nothing, he deceives himself. But let each one test his own work, and then his reason to boast will be in himself alone and not in his neighbor. For each will have to bear his own load. (Galatians 6: 1-5)

Summary: It is important to have someone in your life who will speak the truth to you whether you wanted to hear it or not. I tried to blame my employer for my unhappiness, but in reality, it was my own fault for not listening to God and following the path that He made for me. Once I had a good talking-to, I realized that God had never let me down before, and if I followed His path and His will, He will provide a way.

Scenario: Think of a time when you tried to blame someone else for a mistake that you made.

LESSON: BE ACCOUNTABLE FOR YOUR OWN ACTIONS

Questions:

1. How did you recognize that you were the one at fault?

2. Were you able to go back and correct your mistake? If not, why?

3. What did you learn from your mistake?

4. Do you have someone in your life who can hold you accountable for your actions?

LESSON: DON'T SETTLE FOR ANYTHING LESS THAN GOD'S BEST

Chapter 10: Don't Settle

Scripture Verse: Do not be conformed to this world, but be transformed by the renewal of your mind, that by testing you may discern what is the will of God, what is good and acceptable and perfect. (Romans 12:2)

Summary: At one time or another, we are all tempted to settle for less than God's best. I share a story about a time when Renita and I were tempted to do just that. We had finally settled into a nice home, had great careers, and overall had a very pleasant life in the Washington, DC area when things began to unravel at Julia's school. We knew that Julia had the ability to compete and do well in school but others wanted her to settle where she was and to conform to her current environment. We could have left her where she was, but we chose to follow God's direction and look for something better.

Scenario: Think of a time that you struggled with a decision that would require great effort on your part.

LESSON: DON'T SETTLE FOR ANYTHING LESS THAN GOD'S BEST

Questions:

1. Why was the decision difficult?

2. Were you the only one involved or did it affect someone else?

3. Do you feel guilt over your decision?

4. If you made a decision that affected someone else, how did it make them feel?

5. If the situation was reversed and someone was making a decision for you, what would you want them to do?

LESSON: EMBRACE CHANGE

Chapter 11: The Move to Texas

Scripture Verse: And the word of the Lord came to him: "Depart from here and turn eastward and hide yourself by the brook Cherith, which is east of the Jordan. You shall drink from the brook, and I have commanded the ravens to feed you there." (1Kings 17:2-4)

Summary: In this chapter, I describe the decision to make a major change in our lives. I share how one decision impacted our careers, our home, and the direction of our lives.

Scenario: Think of a time where you were forced to make a major change because of something that you believed in.

Questions:
1. Was the change difficult?

2. Did you face condemnation from your family, friends, or coworkers?

LESSON: EMBRACE CHANGE

3. How did it make you feel?

4. As you moved forward, did someone or something help you along the way?

LESSON: REMEMBER TO SERVE OTHERS FIRST

Chapter 8: Understand what is Important

Scripture Verse: In all things I have shown you that by working hard in this way we must help the weak and remember the words of the Lord Jesus, how he himself said, 'It is more blessed to give than to receive.'" (Acts 20:35)

Summary: As parents, we are responsible for raising our children according to God's word. In many cases, we put their interests ahead of our own. After Julia was born, Renita and I made a choice to put Julia first by adjusting our lives to create an environment where Julia could thrive. We changed careers and moved to different cities in order to establish a foundation from which Julia would later soar. We moved from Cincinnati to St. Louis and then to the Washington, D.C. area all within the course of one year to find the right services for Julia. We also discovered that if we took action to fulfill our purpose, God would make a way.

Scenario: Think of a time when you needed to make a major change in your life.

LESSON: REMEMBER TO SERVE OTHERS FIRST

Questions:

1. Were you unsure of making the change or were you certain in the direction that you should go?

2. In making the decision, were you filled with fear or did you have a sense of peace?

3. Did you listen to your "friends" around you, or did you do what you knew was right?

4. When you took action did things seem to "magically" fall into place?

LESSON: SEEK WISDOM

Chapter 7: Seeking Wisdom

Scripture Verse: Ask, and it will be given to you; seek, and you will find; knock, and it will be opened to you" (Matthew 7:7).

Summary: In this chapter, I discover that I needed additional knowledge in order to better help Julia. Renita, and I needed to learn about medical terminology, available resources and how to be better advocates for Julia. We found that the best way to gain knowledge was by simply asking questions. People are more than willing to share their knowledge; all you have to do is ask.

Scenario: Think of a time when someone close to you needed something, but you didn't know how to help.

Questions:
1. Did you actively search for answers?

2. Did you shy away because you thought that you were not "smart enough" to accomplish the task?

LESSON: SEEK WISDOM

3. Did the person suffer because of your lack of knowledge?

4. What would you now do differently if you had the chance?

LESSON: HAVE COURAGE

Chapter 9: Having Courage

Scripture Verse: For God so loved the world, that he gave his only Son, that whoever believes in him should not perish but have eternal life. (John 3:16)

Summary: In this chapter, I describe the feeling that I had in leaving Cincinnati and moving back to my hometown of Washington, D.C. I describe how we sacrificed our home, business, and independence for Julia to attend the school that was the best fit for her. I knew that it was the right thing to do, but it still took courage on our part to go forward.

Scenario: Think of a time where you were faced with a difficult choice.

Questions:
1. Did it require you to make a sacrifice for someone else?

2. Why was the decision difficult?

LESSON: HAVE COURAGE

3. What did you decide to do?

4. Looking back, do you still agree with the decision or do you regret it?

LESSON: INTEGRITY COMES FIRST

Chapter 18: Having Faith

Scripture Verse: The righteous who walks in his integrity—blessed are his children after him! (Proverbs 20:7)

Summary: I learned about the lesson of Integrity early in life learning from my parents. I share how the lessons that I learned growing up helped me to understand that if I do the right things for the right reasons then everything would work out fine. Later on, I learned that many of the lessons my parents taught me actually originate from the Book of Proverbs. The best thing that I learned is that by living a life of integrity and following His path, God always delivers on His promises. We just have to have faith.

Scenario: Think of a time that you did something that you are less than proud of.

Questions:
1. Why did you do it?

2. What did it cost you in terms of time, money, and reputation?

LESSON: INTEGRITY COMES FIRST

3. Would you have been more successful if you were honest?

4. Have you ever asked for forgiveness?

LESSON: BE PASSIONATE ABOUT YOUR PATH

Chapter 19: A New Chapter

Scripture Verse: Whatever you do, work heartily, as for the Lord and not for men. (Colossians 3:23)

Summary: When I made the decision to return to Austin full-time, I didn't focus on what I could get but what I could give. By doing so, I was able to find a new calling. I talk about joining Keller Williams Realty but struggling to find my way. I tried going down a "proven" path but soon realized that it wasn't for me. By reading God's word and using the gifts that God already gave me, I had everything that I needed to be successful. I became passionate about following the path that God had for me. I was able to pursue my purpose and follow my new calling with clarity. When I began to follow His path and not my own, I finally experienced peace.

Scenario: Think about the decisions that you made over the past year?

LESSON: BE PASSIONATE ABOUT YOUR PATH

Questions:

1. Did you make these decisions based on what others thought or what God placed on your heart?

2. Are you happy with the decisions or are you filled with regret?

3. What is stopping you from going back and making a change?

And he said to them, "Go into all the world and proclaim the gospel to the whole creation. Whoever believes and is baptized will be saved, but whoever does not believe will be condemned."

MARK 16:15-16 (ESV)

www.ingramcontent.com/pod-product-compliance
Lightning Source LLC
Chambersburg PA
CBHW021123300426
44113CB00006B/267